THE
EXECUTIVE
CONNECTION

CAROLINE SHAFFER WESTERHOF

THE
EXECUTIVE
CONNECTION

MAYORS and PRESS SECRETARIES
— THE NEW YORK EXPERIENCE —

Dunellen
New York/London

International Standard Book Number: 0-8046-7090-0
Library of Congress Catalog Card Number: 73-88999
Printed in the United States of America

Foreign Representative:
Martin Robertson & Company Ltd.
16 Quick Street, London.

CONTENTS

THE
EXECUTIVE
CONNECTION

ONE

INTRODUCTION

The press secretary of most city mayors originally served to invite news correspondents for personal interviews. However, very few interviews were arranged, except perhaps for a few favored reporters òr leading journalists. Thus the press secretary could exert a great personal influence on the newspapers and encouraged cronyism. Of course, this would no longer be possible, for the media are now characterized as serving as the watchdog of the people, and cronyism is avoided. Currently, government procedures for imparting information have become increasingly professional. And information officers now participate in the formulation of programs and policies, communicate with government decision-makers, and relay information in the same way that they offer knowledge of the policies of government to the people. It is without doubt that the recognition of the press, involving all the media, is an essential element in any government administration.

In the nineteenth century, New York City's administration utilized the newspaper as a political adjunct. Some mayors recognized that good public relations could be a useful tool for influencing public opinion. These early mayors worked directly with the press, employing only the rudiments of an official staff system which worked on a personal, intimate basis.

Some of the mayors of New York have defined the role of their chief press spokesman, but, more often than not, press relations have not always been planned; rather they were evolved by "who said what to whom," as well as other unforeseeable events. Also press relations have suffered, because many of the mayors of New York have not set up well-defined goals or the means to accomplish them, and there is still administrative confusion prevalent in the thinking concerning the role and functions of the press secretary to the mayor. Professor Wallace Sayre has noted:

A mayor must depend primarily upon himself in his role as chief of state. The institutionalization of the role is still quite rudimentary and the forms of assistance are specialized rather than comprehensive. The press secretary occupies the central staff position for this role, but his interests tend to focus upon the mayor's relationships with the communication media, upon press releases, press conferences, radio and television appearances by the mayor. The state which the press secretary has constantly in mind is thus an important but restricted aspect of the mayor's responsibilities as the chief of state. The deputy mayor in some administrations has also assisted the mayor in the chief-of-state role . . . .

Being poorly conceived of by mayors, the chief-of-state function has quite naturally been poorly staffed and poorly managed. Thus, for example, the mayor's press conferences (if they may be called such) have evolved in forms more convenient to the press than to serve the purposes of the mayor. They are unscheduled, unplanned episodes, the initiative as to time and constant belonging more often to the press corps than to the mayor. The morning's news stories and editorials more often set the day's agenda for the mayor and his associates than do the mayor and his staff. In most of their relations with the press, most mayors are "off-balance" and on the defensive much of the time.[1]

The City of New York is presently one of the most populous cities in the world, and the views its mayor holds, accordingly, are deemed significant not only to the people of the city but to professional politicians across the country and overseas. As the prestige of the office of the mayor of New York City has grown, mayors have become increasingly depen-

dent on the functions of the press secretary to abet the twin
pressures of desire to talk (by mayors) and the desire to
listen by a large audience.

The press secretary is the most important of the mayor's
staff in terms of articulating, advising on, and communicating
policy, as well as being available to serve as a personal,
public, and professional liaison with the "real world." The
press secretary must (a) disseminate information about policy
making (b) influence the course of public policy (c) increase
the mayor's personal, political, and professional influence and
power and (d) strengthen the mayor's image or change it
where necessary, so that the public's perception is the best
possible for the mayor to effect his personal and political
goals.

One of the most difficult demands made of a press secretary
is that he be on duty twenty-four hours a day. He must be
instantly available to offer the news media the feeling of being
witness to situations as they unfold. Consequently, the press
officer must demonstrate organizational skill to marshall
forces for the executive; he must quickly interpret information
so the media can easily convert it into finished copy, accurately
and in time to meet deadlines.

The press secretary to a mayor must learn to temper the
wording of direct commands the mayor will make, and he
must be sensitive to and cognizant of impending political
danger to the mayor if a particular course of action were
pursued.

The press secretary hopefully expresses policies the mayor
puts forth in clearly defined terms designed for maximum
comprehension. He also must express political goals clearly.
To do this successfully requires expeditious and proper distribution of statements to the media, the proper handling of
information, and establishment of rapport with reporters—all
to win the understanding and support of groups that are
concerned and involved with the political process. This
ultimately means that the press secretary must comprehend
every issue thoroughly and must be aware of possible situations

that might arise. If the press secretary fails to meet these demands of his office properly, the result could be a lack of understanding between the part of the press and public, poor public relations, and an overall mayoral credibility gap.

The office of the press secretary is not listed on any official mayoral and city organizational chart. (Within most administrative and organization structures it is often considered to be a step-child in bureaucracy. Also it is sometimes overlooked, because the press secretary's job usually does not run smoothly; it is not a "neat" organization with efficient techniques of administration, which is repellent to many who allege that there should be an orderly, systematic approach to all aspects of administrative science.) Sometimes the office is de-emphasized to encourage the public to believe that the actions of the secretary really are those of the mayor (which they should be). This means that the mayor and the press secretary must establish and maintain a close rapport and trust. The mayor must be able to rely on his press secretary to decide what information should be made available to the public and what may be legitimately withheld. The press secretary in turn must be of such character that his statements to the public will always be accepted as being reliable. The position of press secretary above all incorporates extensive power rooted solely in trust, without statutory reliance of any kind.

The press secretary to a mayor may have to function in relation to all phases of the administrative process, including participation in planning and implementing policies. This study has revealed that the press secretary can have a strong influence on the decisions the mayor makes.

In large city administrations especially, the press secretary to a mayor also will have to deal with other press secretaries who represent the heads of the various departments of a city administration.

The study has also revealed that the press secretary must have an effective sense of communication through formal channels of reaching the media, and a familiarity through informal channels based on personal and social relationships.

For the purposes of research interviews were arranged with people who have been or still are press secretaries to mayors, and, of course, from printed sources including administrative studies, publications by Mayor Lindsay of New York City, press secretaries, such as Woody Klein and Oliver Pilat, to earlier mayors, and the papers of past mayors of New York in the Municipal Archives. The press secretary to Mayor Lindsay was personally observed at work. Others interviewed were on the staff of Mayor Lindsay in different positions.

Questions were prepared to collect data and to evaluate the press secretary's office and its functions. Occasionally, questions were modified to meet the particular circumstances of the person being interviewed. Whenever a second interview was held, it was designed to build upon the experience and the findings of the first interview. Those interviewed, aside from press secretaries, included journalists, the wife of a former press secretary, and a special assistant to Mayor Wagner who worked as a speech writer.

I was concerned with such specific questions as: What administrative structures were set up in the Office of the Mayor of New York City to handle press relations? How did the chief press spokesman identify with the elected leader? What were the situations where the mayor and/or his press staff had to choose between competing goals and loyalties? What were the most important effects of the decisions and activities of the press secretary on the mayor, the press, and the public? What were the long-range goals of this office? What were the short-range goals of this office? Should the press chief have been a specialist with expertise in journalism or a political generalist? Should standard practices have been established for the handling of press relations? Could they actually have been established to function on a formal basis? Why must the press be courted so extensively? How important was it from the mayoral viewpoint? How did the press secretary act to support the functioning of the mayor? Has it been possible for communications and press relations to be administered "efficiently," and with "planning, organization, command, coordination and control?"

At the outset, I assumed there is the need for an information office at the executive level of government, developed according to the needs of the executive and the nature of his jurisdiction. For if there is to be greater participation by the public and greater awareness of all people concerning their political systems and their desire to become involved in them, it is essential that the position of press secretary be analyzed fully and completely. Nevertheless a clear majority of the people I spoke with had no comprehension of how to create a mayoral or any other kind of governmental press release, but they did complain of a credibility gap that the press release can be made to overcome. Hopefully, this book will provide an understanding of the office of the press secretary in all its mechanisms for those responsible for running municipality, village, and state governments and give them the opportunity to improve upon their press secretary system or structures.

TWO

THE EARLIEST MAYORS

There always has been some form of relationship between the
mayors of the City of New York and the press, ever since
1898 when the greater New York City was incorporated.
However, the first mayors did not appoint press secretaries
and had no particular press functionaries on staff. They
issued routine announcements themselves. Most of these
mayors were not entirely cognizant of the significance of
broad-based public information policies. Mayors George
McClellan (1903-1909) and William J. Gaynor (1910-1913)
did employ male secretaries who were former newspapermen,
well aware of the importance of the printed word and its distribution to the public. Both were officially listed as
secretary to the Mayor, but they also served as trouble-shooter,
appointments secretary, political secretary, and operational
subchief of staff.

Robert A. Van Wyck was the first mayor of the City of New
York, serving from 1898 to 1901. During his administration
it was well known that the Democratic party Boss Richard
Croker frankly and openly ruled the City of New York as a
dictator and that the mayor had little power. Since the
mayor had no administrative staff member with power to
protect his image, he had to defend his policies and counter

abuse and attacks made upon him in his official capacity in
direct confrontation with the press.

As a result, the *New York Times* observed on January 5,
1889 that:

So great a part of the Mayor's message is given up to a confused
and floundering exposition of the financial affairs of the city that he is
able to devote but meagre space on recommendations of things that
ought to be done for the good of the city.

There did not appear to be any direct press relationship or
a need to create headlines to develop any favorable public
opinion. The relationship between the executive and the
newspaper reporters was not only informal but quite casual.
Van Wyck's activities were recorded in somewhat sensation-
alized interpretative reports rather than as factual statements:

Van Wyck . . . skated on very thin ice when he and his great friend,
John F. Carroll bought a large interest in the American Ice Company
and then excluded all rivals from the use of city docks. The so-called
"ice scandal" was the last nail in Van Wyck's political coffin, for the
newspapers made the most of it, called him the "ice man," and
charged that he was making a fortune at the expense of the tenement
dwellers in the city.[1]

Syrett further observed that "according to a reporter Van
Wyck got drunk on his last day in office, and he drew few
sober breaths from that day until the day he died."

Mayor Van Wyck had little contact with the press and
accordingly received little press attention and newspaper
commentary. Much of the attention he was given was not
favorable, as can be seen from the statements quoted above.

History does not record much direct information regarding
the use of the press by Mayor Seth Low who served for only
one year between 1902 and 1903. However, on February
19, 1885, Seth Low, as mayor of Brooklyn, had delivered an
address in which he recognized the significance of the news
media.

I can recall the time when it was impossible to take up the evening papers in our city or almost impossible without finding there some communication from one of the heads of departments charging another with failing to sustain him in this or that. I have seen controversies carried on in the public press between the mayor of the city and heads of departments as to whose fault it was that this or that trouble remained unremedied . . .

Further, recognizing the importance of public opinion in charter revision politics Mr. Low stated "This charter was not obtained by us very quickly, nor as the result of a hasty thought and purpose, but we worked towards it for six years, until public opinion in both parties was almost unanimous in favor of us trying this sort of an instrument; and I think public opinion was never more unanimous in its favor than it is today, after it has been in operation for three years and a little more."[2]

Mayor Low's speeches about the administration of government and the responsibility of the mayor and the people included numerous references to the press and the need to cultivate public opinion.

In every direction the opportunity for a city to benefit its citizens by a government able to command complete popular confidence is beyond description.[3]

Also, he utilized the press for making public announcements.

Proclamation of the Mayor, May 7, 1903, May 24-May 30: During the whole of this week, the citizens are requested to fly their flags . . . the newspaper press of the city is asked to bring home to the people a sense of New York's long history.[4]

He gave weekly talks, such as the "Weekly Talk No. 8 of the Honorable Seth Low, Mayor of the City of New York, related to assessing real estate at value prescribed by law," before the City Real Estate Board on September 25, 1902. It was printed in the Martin B. Brown press book.

He made designations of newspapers to announce various public notices that affected the people of New York City. The following are examples:

February 17, 1902: I designate the *New York Times* and the *Evening Post* as the two daily newspapers in which public notice of the time and place of such hearing shall be given by publishing notice thereof on

February 18 and 19, 1902. (This was a public hearing regarding the amending of the Greater New York Charter.) . . .[5]

February 27, 1902: I designated the *New York Times* and *Commercial Advertiser* hearing on account for relief of Eugene F. Vacheron, for work, labor, services and materials furnished and rendered to the City of New York.[6]

He also issued notices to the *Mail,* the *Express,* the *World,* and the *Jamaica Daily Standard,* among others.

One letter published in the press indicates what the mayor wished to have published by the news media.

By virtue of this law, the public sale of liquor has been stopped and a peaceable and orderly Sunday has been already more perfectly secured, since the first of January, as I judge from the public press, than certainly at any time for four years past.

Because, however, it may be very possible, as you imply, to buy liquor in many saloons behind closed doors on Sunday, it pleases you to say, in effect, that the law is treated by the ad as though it did not exist.

Read, however, in the light of the interview with the honored President of your Society, which appeared in the "Mail and Express" on the twentieth instant, it bears a very different aspect. In that interview, Dr. Parkhurst said; "It impresses me that the present excise law will be exceedingly hard to enforce. . . ."[7]

The mayor did have his problems with the press, however. One letter of his records:

January 10, 1902: letter by secretary to Mr. Rudolph Rubens regarding misstatements in clippings . . . and would be pleased to explain it . . .[8]

But Mayor Low did incur problems in his dealings with the press. For one, he had the problems of a story being released to the press before the involved parties were informed. The secretary to the mayor wrote the following to the Rev. Charles H. Parkhurst on January 23, 1902:

My dear Dr. Parkhurst:

Mayor Low directs me to say that he regrets that inadvertently his reply to you was given to the press before the original copy was placed in your hands. In order that you may not fail to receive it today, I am sending it to your house.[9]

Mayor Seth Low had demonstrated early in his political career that he understood the need for press coverage and communicating to the public through the media, although he did not assign a press functionary.

George B. McClellan was mayor of New York from 1903 to 1909. He has been a newspaper reporter in his younger years and had become sensitive to the manipulation and pressures the press could apply. Prior to having won the mayoral election, Mr. McClellan continuously used the press as a medium for the dissemination of his ideas. McClellan's autobiography (edited by Harold C. Syrett and published in 1956) reveals his continuous regard, understanding, concern, and interest for the printed word, and he was aware of the best timing for submitting newspaper copy. Both his and President Theodore Roosevelt's methods had been "to take advantage of the thinness of the Monday paper after the quiet of the traditional Sabbath by releasing something on Sunday in time to be seized eagerly by the news-starved editor making up his front page for the next day."[10]

McClellan looked for bright young newspapermen in making some of his appointments. He appointed John H. O'Brill, a former newspaperman, as his Executive Secretary, who became more of an administrative aide and sophisticated errand boy. He was appointed on the recommendation of Edward G. Riggs of the *Sun.*

It was some time after I took office before my office staff was running smoothly. John H. O'Brill was an ideal mayor's secretary. He was a good executive, wrote really excellent English, was good-looking with good manners, and was a perfect and successful buffer between the mayor and the public. I appointed as clerk in the charge of the records, a nice-looking young graduate of Manhattan College recommended by Murphy. It was not long, however, before O'Brill discovered that so as to save himself trouble, he was filing the records by the simple process of throwing them into the wastebasket.[11]

O'Brill also acted as McClellan's campaign aide during his bid for reelection. Since Democratic party Boss Murphy did not support McClellan's bid for reelection, McClellan had to rely on O'Brill's assistance.

Without Murphy to rely on, I was obliged, with O'Brill's very efficient help, to map the strategy and carry the speaking of the campaign entirely on my own shoulders.[12]

As newsworthy events took place, Mayor McClellan himself would simply call reporters into his office. He recalled that the day he took the oath of office "after the handshaking was over I returned to the inner office, summoned the press and announced my cabinet, after which I swore them in, and sent them on their way rejoicing to take over their departments."[13]

McClellan enjoyed the camaraderie and warmth of newspaper reporters, and he knew how to cultivate them. These interactions between the mayor and press in this period of history are better understood as a direct relationship. Nevertheless, even he had his difficulties with the newspapers. For example, while he was running for mayor McClellan noted:

The press was almost solidly against me. In fact, the only newspaper that supported me was the *Daily News* .... There was a general disposition to misquote me and not to print my speeches as I delivered them. Accordingly, so as to avoid misquotation, we determined that it would be wise for me to read my speeches on the stump....

The press had been so unwilling to print my 'stuff' that before I delivered my last speech we sent an advance copy to all the morning papers for publication as a paid advertisement, even the *Times* refused to accept it. Afterwards, however, the owner of the *Times* assured me that the speech had been refused through error! ...

On election night his (Hearst's) reporter at my headquarters and a youth on my staff faked a statement from me, signed with my rubber stamp, giving Hearst the entire credit for my election. I at once wrote to Hearst that the statement which he had printed on the front page of the *American* was a fake. He never answered my letter, and I was told, was very angry with me for writing it. I could not, however, allow myself to be put on record as considering myself under such deep obligations to him. [14]

McClellan commented on his difficulties with the press at that time:

One of the rules of the game in politics in this country is that a public man must accept newspaper abuse with a smile and not retaliate, for nothing is ever gained by declaring a feud with the press.[15]

However, one incident turned out more favorably for the mayor:

I always followed the *unwritten law* of accepting *newspaper abuse without protest* [emphasis added]. His reply was another scarehead story to the effect that I had tried to sandbag and 'intimidate' him by depriving him of city advertising. As none of the other newspapers paid the slightest attention to the story, neither did I, and within a fortnight the *News* had ceased to exist.[16]

In the election of 1905, McClellan's opponent was publisher William Randolph Hearst, which gave him a unique relationship with newspapers:

Hearst had announced that he would run as the candidate of the Independence League, a party that he had himself organized. (I had also announced that I would seek renomination and reelection.)[17]

. . .

In my fight for reelection I very soon found that Hearst was a far stronger candidate than anyone had supposed that he would be and showed his great ability at making a very effective campaign. He had unlimited money, was a good campaigner, and of course had his newspaper behind him. On the other hand, every other newspaper supported me, with the exception of the *Tribune* which supported the Republican candidate, William M. Ivins, who was running almost openly in Hearst's interest.

Realizing Hearst's strength I had hoped that the Republican convention would endorse me, but Hearst's influence with the Republican bosses was so great that my hope came to nothing. . . .[18]

Hearst had made excellent use of press demagoguery, distortion, and rumors published in his newspapers to win the campaign.

Mayor McClellan continued to have his troubles with Hearst and his newspaper even after being reelected:

Soon after I took office an assemblyman named Jacob D. Remsen introduced a bill to permit the New York Consolidated Gas Company to remove its manufacturing plant from near the Riverside Drive in Manhattan to Astoria in Queens Borough.

Hearst, who after his two days' halfhearted support at the close of
the campaign, had turned against me the day after I took office,
promptly began a crusade against the Remsen Gas Bill on the ground
that as a corporation wanted it, it must be necessarily bad. The *New
York Herald* joined him, and the rest of the press remained neutral . . .
The bill passed the legislature and came before me for the public hearing
required by law. Before the hearing began Thomas F. Ryan came to see
me and told me that Odell, the Governor, had asked him to tell me that
he, Odell, gave me his word that if I signed the bill he would also do so.
This relieved my mind, for as there had been so much newspaper
criticism of the bill, I did not enjoy the prospect of signing it only to
have it vetoed by Odell.[19]

Mayor McClellan also suffered from the power of the
Hearst press when it supported the defeat of a bill in the
state legislature in which the mayor had an interest. The
bill concerned the construction of a new Grand Central
Terminal and the elimination of the tracks on Eleventh
Avenue. Mayor McClellan had asked Senator Martin Saxe, a
Republican from New York County, to introduce the bill.
The Hearst newspapers opposed the bill to such an extent that
Senator Saxe weakened and opposed his own bill, which never
came to a vote.

Said Mayor McClellan, "the Hearst newspapers have much
to answer for in defeating it."[20]

Mayor McClellan also had trouble with Laffan, owner of
the *Sun.*

Laffan turned on me and abused me with great vigor. I stopped sending
the *Sun* advertisements and let it be known that I should take away its
designation unless it ceased attacking me.[21]

. . .

My relations with Laffan went through three phases: when I had his
enthusiastic support, when I had his equally enthusiastic enmity, and
when I had his neutrality. Of the three I greatly preferred the last.
He was so emotional and so extreme that, in supporting me, he overdid
matters, and sometimes by his excessive praise made me ridiculous. His
enmity was equally excessive and while very unpleasant, overshot the
mark and did not do much harm.[22]

The mayor was not treated with much more sympathy by
the editors of the *Evening Post:*

My relations with the *Evening Post*, were to say the least, cool. Villard, its then proprietor, is I think, the most solemn individual I have ever known. If I accomplished anything which has been previously advocated by his paper, he remained silent, if I did anything of which he disapproved he abused me with unrestrained enthusiasm.[23]

At one period he began a crusade against me because of the condition of the street pavements in the Borough of Manhattan. I called the attention of his City Hall reporter to the fact that under the charter the street pavements were under the exclusive jurisdiction of the borough presidents. The next day he printed an editorial demanding that I at once remove the borough president from office. I marked the section of the charter which vests the removal of the borough presidents exclusively in the governor of the state and asked the *Post's* City Hall man to show it to Villard. The only result was a violent editorial abusing me for not using my influence with the governor (which of course was nil, for the governor was a Republican) to have him remove the borough president.[24]

However, the mayor had a better relationship with the *New York Times.*

Louis Wiley, the very able business manager of the *Times* came to me and with perfect correctness asked for the continuance of the *Times* designation. He offered no terms and made no promises. I redesignated the *Times,* and received its loyal and friendly support as long as I was Mayor and have ever since been treated by the *Times* with great friendliness.[25]

. . .

Almost immediately after my election the newspapers that had most violently opposed me began to wave olive branches, and the reason for this was perfectly plain. Under the statute the Mayor designates the newspapers that print the city advertisements. I do not know what the city's printing bill mounts to now, but in my time it ran to nearly $600,000 a year. The city advertisements must be printed in all the Brooklyn newspapers, but in Manhattan the Mayor must designate three papers printed in English of which not more than two may belong to any one party, one paper printed in German, one in Italian, one in French, and one in Yiddish. It was a scandalous state of affairs, and I tried three times to have the law repealed so that the city's printing bill might be kept within bounds. Each time my bill was introduced the newspapers enthusiastically applauded my effort and then used pressure at Albany to prevent the bill being reported out of committee. I think that all this explains the olive branches.[26]

In recollection Mayor McClellan noted that "I never had a good press, for with the exception of the *Times* whose owner and managers were personally my friends, none of them forgave me for having been elected. What support I received from the others was purely perfunctory."[27]   Editor Syrett pointed out, however, that "McClellan fails to mention that, until his break with Murphy following the election of 1906, he was consistently supported by the pro-Tammany *New York Daily News.*"[28]

Mayor McClellan was sensitive to the press' hunger for exploitation of scandal.

Every police scandal that breaks in New York is exploited to the limit by the press which is very prone to compare our force with the Metropolitan Police Force of London to the great disadvantage of our own. When there is a scandal involving the London police, the British press minimize it. The last two London police scandals which were very serious, were investigated by a commission appointed by the Home Secretary from within the force, and this extraordinary procedure failed utterly to appeal to the somewhat eccentric sense of British humor.[29]

A cartoon in the *New York Globe,* March 3, 1904, sarcastically interpreted his attitude. The caption read:

"Say Honestly, Tell me is the Lid on?"

George Washington was looking at Mayor McClellan who was seated on the cover of a barrel wearing a homburg. The lid of the cover is partially lifted. A tiger is on the shelf, and the barrel is labeled "Vice." ... The Gentleman and the Tiger—McClellan and Tammany—was he going to change?

The Mayor's daily agenda to some extent was dictated by the outcries in the press.

The first serious difficulty I had with a department head was at the very beginning of my term. The New York Public Library which was under construction was surrounded by a high board fence. One morning New York awoke to find the fence covered with advertising signs which had been painted during the night and extended around the entire block. Without a single exception the newspapers denounced me as a vandal and very properly demanded that the signs should be painted out. I was as much outraged by the matter as with the newspapers.[30]

McClellan constantly noted the attitude and thinking of the press. He was ever watchful for support or a lack of support as an indication of public opinion.

Thomas F. Ryan strongly urged me to appoint former Superintendent of Police Thomas F. Byrnes. . . . I objected that Byrnes had an exceedingly bad reputation for honesty and that every newspaper in town would be against him. . . .[31]

The mayor also had problems when he dealt with individual reporters, as well as with the newspapers they worked for.

One of the few disagreeable incidents that I ever had with a newspaperman was with a fellow alumnus of Princeton named Louis Lang, of the class of 1881 and of the New York *American.* One morning he came to see me and after "passing the time of day" said, "Mr. Mayor, Mr. Hearst wants to know if you have a corrupt motive in advocating the Remsen Gas Bill?" To which I replied, "Louis, you know better than to ask me a question like that. Get out of my office and don't come back." The next day the *American* carried a "scare headline" across its front page: "Mayor does not deny that he has a corrupt motive in supporting the Remsen Gas Bill," which of course was literally, if not actually true.[32]

In his autobiography, McClellan often revealed his awareness of using the press to arouse public opinion. He states, for example:

. . . and one morning Edward F. Sheppard as counsel for the Pennsylvania came to see me and told me that unless the Aldermen passed the franchise as drawn, arrangements had been made to enact a law at Albany transferring the franchise power from the Aldermen to the Board of Estimate and to pass the bill over my veto should I veto it. I said to him, "Mr. Sheppard, do I understand that this is a threat?" "Yes, Mayor," he replied, "it is a threat. If the Aldermen do not give us our franchise, their powers will be taken away from them, and you will not be able to prevent it." I then said, " That being the case, Mr. Sheppard, I wish you a very good morning," and showed him the door. When I saw the newspapermen I told them of my interview without mentioning Sheppard's name. The papers were frankly skeptical and demanded that I name the man who had threatened me, for the Pennsylvania, for various reasons, had had the friendship of almost all in New York newspapers. When I gave them Sheppard's name, they were still skeptical until Sheppard acknowledged the truth of my statement, after which they remained silent. . . .

By this time I had succeeded in arousing a good deal of public opinion in support of my position and Murphy found it impossible to control any votes in the Board of Estimate except those of the presidents of Manhattan, Bronx and Queens, and with only four votes at his disposal he was helpless.[33]

. . .

Mrs. Russell Sage very generously gave the city one of the finest collections of rhodendra in the world and selected as the site for its installation the eastern side of Central Park on Fifth Avenue. The old lady and I with much pomp planted the first bush. Unfortunately, the newspapers played up the little ceremony with the result that more than half the plants had been stolen.[34]

. . .

The panic of 1907 brought me for the first time into close relations with J. P. Morgan, the elder. . . .

During the summer of 1907 I was on my vacation in the Adirondacks when I received a telegram from the deputy and acting comptroller saying that an issue of fifteen million dollars of city bonds which he had advertised had failed to receive a single bid, and appealing to me for help.[35]

It was then suggested that Mayor McClellan meet with J. P. Morgan, the financier, which was then arranged.

"How much do you want?" asked Morgan. I answered that I thought twenty-five million dollars would answer for the present. "Offer forty million dollars in your advertisement," said Morgan. "But, my dear sir," I replied, "if we failed to get bids for fifteen million dollars how can we possibly hope to sell forty millions?" "Leave that to me," replied Morgan. "If you don't get any bids, I give you my word that I will give you my personal check for the whole amount." I expressed my sincere appreciation of his public spirit and then asked him what I should say if questioned by the press. He said, "Leave everything to me. Say nothing. Just get out your ad as soon as possible, and I will do the rest."

When City Hall reporters asked me whether there was any truth in the rumor that Morgan had agreed to underwrite the next issue of city bonds, I replied that I had nothing to say. When he was asked the same question he replied, "I decline to deny or affirm the rumor." When the bids for the forty million dollars issue were opened, they were found to have been oversubscribed three times, the firm of J. P. Morgan and Company not bidding.[36]

. . .

As another example, for the smooth working of the government it was absolutely necessary to have supporters at Albany, not only to get through the legislation that was required but to prevent "strikes" on the city treasury. On matters of legislation, as well as on questions of ethics, Murphy and I seldom if ever saw eye to eye. It was impossible to keep clear of politics if I were to accomplish results. *There were those who urged me to reply on the force of public opinion* [emphasis supplied] in a righteous cause. Unfortunately, it is difficult, if not impossible, to arouse public opinion on any issue short of one involving a great question of public morale. Besides as I was always requiring legislation, often on very petty matters, I should have been obliged to spend my time in trying to interest the public in mere questions of routine administration.[37]

McClellan also wrote that the opposition of the press had a powerful effect.

During the panic year of 1907 Morgan either took up himself or caused his subsidiary banks to take up over three hundred million of the city's bonds and short term bonds, and by his individual support really saved the city from bankruptcy.

I thought that it would be a graceful gesture to give him the freedom of the city and consulted his son as to whether his father would like it. The younger Morgan told me that Mr. Morgan would be delighted. I sent a message to the aldermen urging them to confer the freedom on him, when Pulitzer began to froth at the mouth declaring that Mr. Morgan had been paid at usurious rates for all that he had done—which was, of course, untrue—and that it would be a scandal to officially thank him. The aldermen were terrified by the attitude of the *World* and could not be persuaded to act on my message. And so Mr. Morgan was never officially thanked by the city whose credit he had saved.[38]

McClellan noted that the support of the press also could be a powerful influence.

Morgan's methods were extremely direct, and he was always surprised if he did not get what he wanted on demand. He called me up one day and asked if the New York and Westchester Railroad had applied for a franchise. When I answered that it had, he said, "I want that franchise granted today." I explained that that was impossible, and that the law required a public hearing, and that the proposed form of franchise that had been submitted was quite unsatisfactory to the city. He grunted and said, "Always the damned law. I think that you might oblige me." I found out afterwards that certain individuals interested in the franchise had, without Morgan's knowledge, made a deal with Murphy to have it put through exactly as drawn and to pass it over my veto. *The press supported me valiantly* [emphasis added] in my fight so that, when finally granted, the franchise was perfectly satisfactory to the city but by no means satisfactory to its proponents.[39]

After the fashion of the day, McClellan served as his own press secretary. He had a good appreciation that the news media was the most important primary means of disseminating information. He knew well its usefulness in generating favorable public opinion and in getting his image before the public. He was also particularly sensitive to partisan reporting and understood its destructive and positive powers. Because he was a former newspaperman, he was familiar with the profession's techniques and tactics and had been cognizant that a close relationship with the newspaper reporters and publishers was essential for the functioning of the mayor's office. From his sense of timing, his use of the press, and his recognition of his own needs, McClellan unwittingly defined the role of the press secretary.

Mayor William J. Gaynor, the fourth mayor of New York City, served from 1910 to 1913, during the city reform period. His early achievements evoked much comment and applause from the press. He became good news copy as well, because the public became fascinated by his pungent personality and his unorthodox behavior, which the newspapers revealed through published letters the mayor sent to them. Syrett quoted former Mayor McClellan on this practice.

Gaynor was a most peculiar and eccentric man who had the knack of writing rather clever and very insulting letters, with which he terrorized his correspondents, for he always gave his letters to the press and the press will always print anything insulting from or to a public official on the ground that it is news.[40]

Gaynor and his secretary, Adamson, kept a constant eye on the press. When newspapers printed critical stories or editorials, Gaynor was quick to write letters of reproof or

correction. He frequently complained of being misquoted
or misinterpreted and regarded newspaper reporters as
unreliable.

Mayor Gaynor had appointed as his executive secretary,
Robert Adamson, a former journalist who served as a link
between the reporters and the mayor. Though Mayor
Gaynor had written in a letter to W. D. Barbout, on June
9, 1910, "I pay very little regard to what the newspapers
say anyway," the selection of Adamson as his secretary
was calculated to cultivate good press relations. The mayor
actually did most of his own writing, and Adamson was
more of an advisor and distributor of information than an
image-maker and acted as a buffer between the mayor and
reporters. Gaynor was always reluctant to grant interviews,
but when he did grant an interview, he usually insisted
on the presence of a stenographer who took down his
words verbatim in order to reduce the hazard of misquotation. "No Madam," Gaynor said to a reporter for *The
World* after a rare interview, "you have not taken a single
note, and yet you are going to try to put what I have said
to you in quotation marks, and with your shorthand mind
and longhand fingers I fear you will make some mistake and
even get me into trouble."[41]

Thus Adamson publicized Gaynor's activities, speeches
and writings and relied on the letters that flowed out over
the mayor's desk in unbelievable quantity as a rich source
of human interest material in which circulation-conscious
editors delighted. The publicity-minded mayor and his
ex-newspaperman saw that City Hall reporters were well
supplied with copy.

Recognizing that citizen awareness and support must be
cultivated, Secretary Adamson also compiled and prepared
a "manual of the city government, giving information about
the officials and their duties and city affairs in general."[42]
The *New York Times* editorialized:

This is the first attempt to put before the citizens a manual of
information concerning the city government ... Mr. Adamson himself

outlines in *The Year Book* another excellent plan for bringing information on municipal affairs to the attention of a greater number of
citizens. Instead of the unorganized reports which the City Record
prints and is pretty dry stuff to the average reader, Mr. Adamson
proposes a central control over all municipal reports and bulletins,
making an effort not only to discard irrelevant detail but also to
present information by means of charts, graphs and maps. Teaching
the New Yorker facts about the conditions in his own city will do
more than anything else towards awakening civil spirit.[43]

Gaynor was careful that his speeches were reported in
the press. He sometimes sent the *New York Times* a copy
of a speech, requesting that it be printed in full in the
Sunday edition, when circulation was the largest.[44] For
example, when he spoke at Annapolis one time he arranged
for the local newspaper to supply his speech to the Associated Press.[45] This practice was not without its problems,
one of which arose when an extemporaneous speech he
gave to the New York Chamber of Commerce was printed
in the Chamber's monthly bulletin. He scolded the
organization's secretary for not submitting the proof to
him.[46]

At Yale University on May 7, 1912 Mayor Gaynor had
said,

Strangely enough every time I say anything on the subject on which
I speak to you tonight, I see great headlines the next day in that
sort of newspaper which you have down in New York ... "The
Mayor advocates the recall of the judiciary" when I have never said
a word to that effect ...[47]

Although the press and public were generally lavish in
their praise of Gaynor's initial accomplishments at City
Hall, they did criticize him at times. It was however not
easy to be critical of Gaynor in the first successful months
of his administration. But the Hearst papers, the morning
American and *Evening Journal*, managed to find something.
The *Journal*, for example, scores Gaynor's appointments
by automatically linking them with Tammany politicians;
its banner headline of March 31, 1910, reading "Mayor
Giving Best Places to Tammany Men." An enterprising

Hearst reporter had written this story. Charles Murphy, leader of Tammany, had been vacationing at Mount Clemens, Michigan. Letters he had received from Gaynor had been thrown into a waste basket and then recovered by a reporter. These letters were used to attempt to show the Tammany link to Gaynor. In April of the same year one of the Hearst men also managed to make a photographic copy of a warrant for $48,000 to be paid by the city to Daniel F. Cohalan, Tammany man and friend of Charles F. Murphy. Indeed, a check had been drawn in favor of Cohalan by Charles Hyde, but he had actually only been issuing a check to pay what had already been established as a claim against the city. Nevertheless, on April 15, Hearst's *American* printed a facsimile of the Cohalan warrant on the front page that was complete in all details except the date of the warrant, December 31 or the date it had been audited by the comptroller, December 29. The body of the article, supported by the undated facsimile, inferred that payment was made by Gaynor and was Tammany's price for giving him the mayoral nomination. The next day the *American* mentioned on an inside page that the dates had been omitted inadvertently in the reproduction process, but that the transaction *had* taken place after Gaynor was mayor.[48]

Gaynor was to have his "day in court" at a joint banquet of the Associated Press and the American Newspaper Publishers' Association held at the Waldorf Astoria Hotel on the night of April 28, 1910. Gaynor spoke before an assemblage that included 600 editors and publishers from all over the nation, including the President of Princeton University, Woodrow Wilson. Herbert F. Gunnison of the *Brooklyn Eagle,* Chairman of the Dinner Committee had invited Gaynor to address the diners on the subject "The Press in Its Relation to Public Officials." Gunnison urged the mayor to speak freely. "The result . . . was a little more than we might have expected."[49]

Gaynor reviewed the facts in the Cohalan case and displayed the Hearst facsimile and then the original warrant to the diners. On the original, the dates were visible in large bold characters: on the facsimile there were blanks where the dates should have appeared. Then he displayed a photograph of the warrant that he had made, where the dates were plainly visible. "The truth is" the mayor said, "I am assured that the dates were actually cut out of the plate with a routing machine. . . Hearst," he said, "had committed two prison felonies, forgery and falsification of a public document."

Gaynor continued his address:

I mention this matter to you because right here is where it should be mentioned. And let me add that it concerns you, the publishers and editors of the decent newspapers far more than it concerns me. If you can stand such things in your great profession the rest of us can stand it, or will try to stand it, until the hour arrives when we shall make up our minds to utterly destroy it, and take effective measures to that end. It is high time that these forgers and libelers were in State's prison, and the time is not far distant when some of them will be there. And just think of a man who is capable of doing things like this being possessed with the notion that he is fit to hold any office from Mayor to President of the United States. Morally speaking, his mind must be a howling wilderness.[50]

The speech was published in all the newspapers of the city, and Hearst started libel suits against the *New York Times,* the *Brooklyn Eagle,* and the *Associated Press.* The press welcomed the mayor's attack on yellow journalism. The *Evening Post* called the speech "a great public service."[51]

Gaynor's letters also indicated his views of the Hearst press. In one letter, the mayor had discussed the Reno prizefight pictures being shown in the theaters. Theater licenses could be revoked only by judges of the Supreme Court, not by the mayor. The district attorney and the corporation counsel advised the mayor that there was no law forbidding pictures that had been shown for years without objection, as Gaynor had pointedly commented. "But the Hearst newspapers kept on denouncing me for not stopping them. Hearst newspapers went on repeating falsehood and even tried to get up a public meeting to denounce me."

People with disordered minds would cut [Hearst articles] out and send them to me with abuse and threats written on the margin, or else with anonymous letters threatening me. Probably they cared nothing about the pictures, but the particular disorder of their minds was inflamed by reading how bad a man I was . . . printed terrible cartoon of me . . . "The Barker" . . . I was dressed up as a ruffian and standing outside a prize-fight ring twirling a cane and barking for people to go and see the sport. Two men slugging each other, one of them down and bleeding were exposed in the ring . . . I suppose . . . others who read no other newspapers . . . and were naturally inflamed against such a ruffian being a mayor. That was the objective these newspapers had in view, although they printed all the pictures of the fight in the most revolting form . . . I had received a few similar threats when these same newspapers published that we were discharging small employees by taking on expensive ones.

Such journalism is, of course, in absolute defiance of the criminal law and it did not enter my mind to publicly call on the grand juries and the district attorney to protect me from it, but I was weak and feared people would say I was then thin. But the journalistic scoundrels have got to stop or get out, and I am ready now to do my share to that end. They are absolutely without soul. If decent people would refuse to look at such newspapers the thing would right themselves at once. The journalism of New York City has been dragged to the lowest depth of degradation. The grossest railleries and libels, instead of honest statements and fair discussion, have gone on unchecked. One cannot help sympathizing with the decent newspapers. . . .[52]

And Gaynor continued his campaign against the Hearst newspapers. The mayor wrote the Governor of New Jersey, Woodrow Wilson:

We have in this town a proprietor of several newspapers, including one in Yiddish, who thinks himself fit for any and every office that comes along, including the Presidency. . . .

He is now puffing himself up in his publications, and crying down everyone else whom he thinks may be in the way as a candidate. His method is like that of some hogs in a fire or a like emergency, namely to jump upon all others in his way, and bear them down

and trample the hob nails with his shoes into their flesh in his efforts
to save his own carcass.

I write to you only to say that I am glad you do not pay any
attention to this common libeler. He can neither add nor detract
from a man like you.[53]

Wilson replied with respect to the "attacks of the
common enemy, misrepresentation is the penalty which men
in public life must expect in the course of the efforts to
render service. Many who would be of immeasurable value
to public service, but are deterred from entering it because
they shrink from this particular penalty."[54]

Hearst started a political and personal feud marked by
such bitter vituperativeness and general bad taste as has
seldom been witnessed in American city politics. Hearst had
his newspapers at his disposal, and for four years he
mercilessly pilloried the mayor in cartoons, editorials, and
slanted news. Gaynor's public position, however, gave him
an advantage. Most of Hearst's rival editors were only too
glad to print Gaynor's strictures which were many and bitter;
one of Hearst's biographers had said that Gaynor "with a
tongue like acid biting into an etching, was one of the few
enemies ever to get under Hearst's toughened skin."[55]

In the mayoral campaign of 1909, Hearst, convinced that
civic righteousness was not to be served by either Gaynor,
representing Tammany, and Bannard representing the
Republican party, permitted his Independence League,
rechristened the Civil Alliance, to nominate him. He was
not particularly anxious to run, but he felt that, by throwing his support to the fusion candidates for other offices,
there was a good chance that Tammany would be left with
an empty honor—the election of a mayor who would be
powerless with a Board of Estimate united in opposition.

Gaynor reacted by stating that Hearst "had come to New
York from California for reasons well known to a great
many people . . . he was a man," said Gaynor, "who
thought he could buy anything with his '$60,000,000';
he advertised himself as if he were a patent medicine."

Referring to the fact that Hearst had been elected to Congress some years before with Tammany support, he said: "And, oh, dear me, how long since he was on the Tammany ticket! How dainty and how nice, and how delicate is the conscience of this man about the Tammany ticket just at present!" To Hearst's claim that he was defeated for mayor in 1906 through the dishonesty of Tammany election officials, Gaynor remarked: "He said his ballot boxes were stuffed. Every time he does not win it is the same cry, 'framed, ballot boxes stuffed; Murphy did it, Tammany did it!'"[56]

Hearst himself did not do much in the way of replying, but his "hirelings" as Gaynor called them, were kept busy. Arthur Brisbane kept up a steady attack on Gaynor in the Hearst papers. He even succeeded in selling to Joseph Pulitzer, whose *World* papers were Gaynor's strongest supporters, the idea of publishing an editorial written by Brisbane himself, which would attack Gaynor in the *Evening World.* Gaynor promptly entered suit against the *World* for libel. After the mayoral election of 1909, the *World* representatives had to use all their powers of persuasion to get Gaynor to withdraw the suit.[57]

Mayor Gaynor also had his arguments with other newsmen. In discussing the subway contracts, the mayor wrote to his friend, Edward C. Blum, a partner in Abraham and Straus, "the falsehood and clamor and low-bred manners of these two or three newspaper proprietors, do not affect us in the least."[58]

With regard to the subway system's operation, Gaynor had noted that "certain newspapers laid down the manner in which we should do it and because we didn't see it our duty to do it the way they told us we must do it . . . we had to endure the abuse of these scoundrels . . . you know whom it includes, unless you don't read these filthy newspapers at all."[59]

When the final hearing was held at the Board of Estimate, Mayor Gaynor noted that:

Five . . . people maybe they were mental defectives passed before us
comparing us to Boss Tweed—the fellow pulled their editorials out of
his pocket to show why he was doing it. The moral assassin is worse
than the physical assassin, especially these poor mentally deficient
people who read these things and take them seriously.[60]

. . .

. . . Newspapers of that kind will tell you what to do and if you don't
do it they will try to blackmail you into doing it. If you don't do it
they will abuse you. Some will come to you with articles and ask how
much is it worth to you not to publish it in that paper. You will
encounter all these things but you will have to stand up against them.
There is nobody on this earth more despicable than the man who
comes into public office and gives what the newspaper dictates. That
is not government.

The same may be said of a man who gives way to clamor of any
kind, especially if it is newspaper clamor or created by newspaper.
Your children in school and colleges . . . will have to see these things in
the papers about you, and be twitted about it. . . . Men are staying out
of public life on account of it.[61]

Once again, in a letter, dated July 11, 1913, he was
castigating newspaper writers.

The degradation of newspaper writers—the present position of newspaper writers, and especially of those who write the news—is degrading
to the last degree. They are mere slaves . . . dishonorable slaves.

The corrupt newspaper proprietor browbeats them and kicks them
about as he sees fit. He does not leave them free to write the honest
truth, but dictates to them that they must lie, garble, forge, steal, or
do anything to write down the official or person who is the subject of
the animosity . . . And if they refuse to do it they are kicked out.
How long will the newspaper writers continue to allow themselves to
be degraded in that way? . . . am acquainted with the young men who
serve as reporters here at the City Hall. They are, as a rule, fine young
fellows. But some of them have to come around to my office shame-
facedly to get the news only to forge and pervert it in the way which
I have said. I pity them. They do not want to do it. They have to do
it or get out. It seems to me the newspaper writers ought to protect
themselves at least to the extent that typesetters, pressmen, and
other mechanics protect themselves. At all events, they ought to band
together and protect themselves against the degradation of being made
to write falsehood and abuse.[62]

Mayor Gaynor, because of these feelings, treated newspaper
reporters in a perfunctory manner; for example,

When a reporter would follow him to his week-end farm at St. James, Long Island, the mayor would appear at the door in answer to the ring, glance at the proffered press card and hand it back with the brusque reply, "Never heard of you. I suggest you get the hell off my front porch."[63]

The newspapers, of course, responded to the attitude Mayor Gaynor had taken to defend himself from newspaper reports made against him in the first place. The *Times* remarked after his nomination:

His continued participation in the strifes of politics, his recklessness of speech, and his frequent appeals to unreasoning and dangerous passion while holding the high office of judge of the Supreme Court, have for years constituted a scandal that has been deplored and denounced by right-thinking men.[64]

The *Tribune* thought Gaynor was "an agitator rather than an administrator" and found it necessary to speak severely of his "boorishness, vulgarity and profanity."[65] The *Sun* which would probably have denounced George Washington as a dangerous agitator had it been published in his day, continuously sniped at Gaynor. On the day after his nomination in 1913 the *Sun* editorialized: "A worse man than Judge Gaynor might have been chosen, but it would have entailed a good deal of trouble to find him." As the campaign progressed, the paper's opinion remained unchanged: how bad a man he could be once he let himself go.[66] He found no friends either on the *Evening Post,* the traditional enemy of all things emanating from the Tammany headquarters (Fourteenth Street Wigwam).

Gaynor, in turn, was goaded by the libelous and scurrilous attacks and his always edgy temper often got out of control. Many of his speeches consisted almost wholly of shouted epithets interspersed with unbecoming self-praise. A typical gesture was his reply to a malicious letter sent to him by a fusionist worker, one A. B. Kerr; where the typist had written the name of the addressee, he crossed out "Kerr" and substituted "Cur."[67]

However, the editorial opposition heaped upon candidate
Gaynor during the campaign changed within six months to
praise for Mayor Gaynor (that is, almost all changed, with
the exception of Hearst). For example in the magazine
section of the Sunday *Times,* there appeared shortly after
the nominating convention a resume of Gaynor's career
showing the writer had grasped that beneath the violence
of his expressions, Gaynor displayed sound principles.
Everything he had done on the bench and off the bench
pointed to a strong Jeffersonian philosophy: "That government is best which governs least."[68] The writer spoke of
those who heard Gaynor's speech as voiceless people who did
not write to editors or otherwise make their opinions known.

Gaynor revealed other strong feelings about the press. At
a speech at the dinner of the Politics Club of Columbia
University on March 13, 1913, in an address entitled
"Advice on Entering Politics" Gaynor said,

The chief obstacle to good government in the city is a corrupt press.
There is nothing that confronts the American people in some part of
this country which requires a remedy more than the license of the
press. . . .

These put in office by you have got to submit to abuse day after
day . . . however they are striving to do their duty. . . . I do not say
that the entire press here are that way, but we certainly have some
that are that way; some in the hands of demagogues and scamps—you
can call them nothing else.[69]

Gaynor had written to Emil W. Kohn in a letter dated
April 1, 1910, "I am able to do very little, except as the
intelligent sentiment of the city sustains me."[70]

Boarding the *Baltic* for a European vacation on September
4, 1913, with, as it turned out, only six days to live, he
said to a reporter, "I am going where you fellows can't get
near me."[71] (He had been wounded by an assassin the last
week of August 1913; several days later he embarked on
his trip to Europe, where he hoped to recuperate.)

On September 3, 1913, he wrote to his sister:

I have not read any newspaper since I was hurt. . . . It is my intention
never to read a line of what has been published in the newspapers about

the matter or me since I was hurt. It might warp my mind about myself. What I am I am, with all my shortcomings, and I am content with that. . . .

I could not bear to have them looking at me in the plight I was in, especially the crowd of newspaper men, and especially those with cameras. Two of them rushed up from the line where they all stood and put their cameras right in my face and snapped them. I finally put my hand up and I think I said "don't." I hope these pictures were not published. The other newspaper men acted decently, as they always do.[72]

The mayor died a few miles off Liverpool, England aboard ship on September 10, 1913.

Mayor Gaynor had preferred not to be written about unless he controlled the news, which he tried to do through his letters to the newspapers or through his public speeches that he required to be printed verbatim.

Gaynor was not helpful to reporters. He was unsympathetic to their responsibilities. Yet he had hired as a personal secretary, Adamson, a man who had been an experienced, news-conscious reporter.

He had observed, while commenting on an argument with Hearst, that:

I have no desire to be a newspaper hero. Newspaper heroes do not last long, those who live by the sword die by the sword and those who live by the newspapers die by the newspapers; that has been my observation.[73]

The relationship between Mayor Gaynor and Secretary Adamson was close and both men understood each other's needs very well. There is no record of conflict and disputation. Secretary Adamson served to transmit to the press his boss' statements. He used press techniques well, but he did not create any of the mayor's policies or statements.

Ardolph Kline became acting mayor upon the death of Mayor Gaynor in September 1913. He served in this capacity for three months and then became a member of Mayor John Mitchel's cabinet. Little has been recorded apparently of Mayor Kline's brief tenure. In one of the few records that

has been made, Kline responded to a news story that he had
considered to be inaccurate, which reported that he intended
to rescind the 1:00 a.m. closing order of cabarets.

This is all rot. I have never said anything or done anything which
would justify such a statement.

This whole story is most unfair. The veiled imputation would be
insulting if it were not ridiculous.[74]

Mayor Kline apparently had no extensive press relations,
although this statement demonstrated he was concerned with
published newspaper criticism.

THREE

JOHN   PURROY   MITCHEL
JOHN   F.   HYLAN

Mayor Mitchel had been nominated by a nonpartisan fusion committee and served from 1914 to 1917. This mayor and his committee used the press extensively in reaching the public before and after the election. His speeches before the Fusion Committee of 107 were printed as major policy statements. For example, the mayor spoke before the Committee on May 2, 1916, delivering his second annual report.

It is essential, therefore, to the success of this experiment in city government for which your Committee of 107 is responsible, that the citizenship of the city should learn from time to time from us and through the authoritative medium of your committee, what this administration had done and what it proposed still to do in discharging the obligations assumed at the election of November 1913. . . .

This annual meeting of your Committee offers the single opportunity to present to the people of the city, in a comprehensive way, the aims and purposes, as well as the accomplishments of those in whom this great public trust of government has been reposed.[1]

In addition to his speech, the mayor distributed to the members of the press, a pamphlet containing his speech printed verbatim. On page 10 of the pamphlet the mayor responded to an attack made on the Department of Charities that had described its deplorable conditions.

Department of Charities had been under storm . . . effort to exercise a much needed supervision of the 23,000 children committed by the city to private charitable institutions . . . administration met by storm of . . . opposition . . . The opposition offered through personal attack in the press and from pulpits throughout the city and later through the agency of the State Board of Charities, suggesting that the city administration was inspired in its work by animum, made it necessary for the City Department of Charities to spread upon the public record the deplorable physical conditions which had been found in certain of these institutions and to state publicly the shocking physical condition of the children.[2]

The mayor acted basically as his own press secretary, and the fact was noted by others with disdain and sadness.

Mayor Mitchel is the poorest man at self-advertising I have ever seen in a conspicuous public position. It is a significant fact that the reporters who cover City Hall swear by Mitchel. The City Hall reporters, en masse, see the mayor each morning. On this especial morning I attended the interview. With typical humorous cynicism the reporter asked "Would you say a few well-chosen words. . . ." The average politician with an eye to keeping in the papers would have jumped at that. Not so Mayor Mitchel. "I haven't a well-chosen word in my system this morning," he replied with a dry smile. . . . So the interview was ended.[3]

Mayor Mitchel's secretary and assistant was Chamberlain Bruere. One of Chamberlain Bruere's responsibilities was the publication of the *1916 Municipal Year Book of the City of New York*. On February 8, 1917, Mayor Mitchel stated:

I believe it is possible from the standpoint of the development of the science of municipal administration, as well as from the standpoint of public education, that a current record be maintained properly describing the structure, functions, and activities of the city government. I trust, therefore, that the precedent now established may be continued to the end that the Year Book may be published annually hereafter.[4]

The Year Book was considered important because,

. . . It takes time in a democracy for facts to sink into the public consciousness . . . takes a long time for public opinion to come to the support of progressive and constructive measures. The people must learn facts, and that takes time; and then they must assimilate them, and they must be able to interpret them gradually.[5]

The mayor obviously was an avid reader of the newspapers and did not rely on Chamberlain Bruere to digest the news for him. There are many examples of the mayor's concern of items and stories he read about in the papers in which he directed the acting mayor to respond for him.

My dear Mrs. Moskowitz,

I have noticed in the newspapers your statement to the effect that your Committee has in its possession evidence against "seven of the most popular and fashionable dancing resorts on Broadway."

It is my wish that immediate action shall be taken upon any evidence coming from a responsible quarter, tending to show either that provisions of law are violated. . . . I shall be grateful, therefore, if you communicate at once the information to which you refer to the Police Commissioner or the Commissioner of Licenses. . . . I feel, as I am sure you will appreciate, that public harm may be done through the publication of general statements based upon evidence not in the possession of the city authorities, unless such evidence is promptly placed at the disposal of those who may properly act upon it.[6]

Mayor Mitchel had a strong belief in the usefulness of the press, and he often used it as a medium to get the facts "straight" before the people. He recognized that, in order to accomplish his work, he needed both the support and criticism of the press. Mayor Mitchel at times gave exclusive interviews to particular newspapers, in one of which, the *Herald,* he told in plain language the reasons for the staggering financial situation with which the city was confronted.

Today for the first time Mayor Mitchel throws aside the clouds of mystery and confusion which have for years enveloped the financial activities of the city, and in an interview given exclusively to the *Herald* . . .[7]

The mayor often delivered major addresses and saw to it that their entire text would be printed in the newspapers. The mayor also announced public statements through the press to be used as notification to the people:

. . . Because of the shortness of time . . . they will take this publication in the press as sufficient notification.[8]

For example, on March 3, 1914, Mayor Mitchel issued a release for the morning papers to "appeal to the people to cooperate during the snow emergency."[9] He also used the press to make administrative announcements, such as a statement to the effect that, because the city had received no increase in state aid, certain departments must reduce their budget. Salaries would also have to be reduced. "If the head of any department desires to take issue with the conclusions of a sub-committee . . . he will have the right of appeal to the Board of Estimate."[10]

Mayor Mitchel felt the press had treated him fairly.

> We who are in the government of the city appreciate the attitude toward us that has been maintained by the press of the city and the country. For myself I may say that attitude has always been essentially a fair one. . . . I have yet to find the time when I can say honestly that I have not been dealt with fairly by the press, and I appreciate that attitude very deeply indeed.[11]

He accordingly was always delighted to attend a dinner of the New York Press Club and welcomed their invitations to be the main speaker.

> . . . Grateful to be here . . . because I am always grateful for the privilege of meeting good friends on an occasion like this, and if I had never felt it before surely I would feel tonight that here I am among friends.[12]

> . . .

> . . . Hopes the Press Club will grow . . . a medium for the social interchange of thought and opinion among the men who control and direct the great force of publicity in this community.[13]

> . . .

> . . . I most of all in public life feel that we need you in our business. . . . Seriously, in order to accomplish the purposes and the works that we have in mind, we need the support and the criticism of the press. We get the criticism very freely, and we get the support sometimes. (There was laughter from the audience at this statement.) We want both because we feel that the real test of successful democratic government is that applied by an intelligent and enlightened public opinion, and we get that expressed through the medium you represent, the press. No one, I think here tonight could fail to be impressed by the power that is represented in this room—the power of these great newspapers of the country.[14]

Julian Street further commented on the newspaper support Mayor Mitchel had received in the city, particularly in looking towards running for reelection.

He is attacked by crooks, cranks, self-seekers, the Hearst newspapers. In appointing heads of departments he tried to find only the best person for the job . . . without being aware of the political faith of the appointee. Because of this there is no party line-up for or against him (unless you call Tammany a party). So also have the newspapers: the Hearst papers are . . . temporarily at least . . . Democratic, and attack him; the *Times* and the *World* are genuinely Democratic and support him; and he is also supported by the violently Republican *Tribune* and the captious *Sun*.[15]

Mayor Mitchel, however, had no liking for the Hearst newspaper machine, and expressed his feelings openly. On one occasion, Mitchel was running for reelection against Judge Hylan in 1917, and during a question-and-answer press interview on October 15, 1917, he stated:

If Judge Hylan wishes to eliminate questions of loyalty and Americanism from this campaign he has a very simple way of doing it. Let him repudiate Hearst and all that Hearst stands for, the doctrine of the Hearst editorials. . . .[16]

Mayor Mitchel often refuted inaccuracies in the press:

The printed statement which you quoted is entirely incorrect. I never said anything of the kind. . . .

I trust that this will make plain to you my position, which, as I said before, from the quoted report of my speech, you have naturally misunderstood.[17]

Sometimes, however, the mayor treated the press with silence. And when he took office on January 1, 1914 he cautioned his new heads of departments to use self-restraint in dealing with the public.

. . . To caution them to self-restraint and to simplicity in their dealings with the public. . . . It will not be necessary for us to go to the people of the city every day to tell them what we propose to do. It will be better for us to wait a little while and then to go to them and tell them what we are going to have done, and to advise with them as to what we shall do further. I would rather have the government of this city for the next few months inconspicuous than have it heralded from day to day in the papers through promises made as to what will be done.[18]

When Mayor Mitchel spoke before the New York Press Club on April 17, 1914, he stated that only when he and his department heads felt policy had been decided upon, would announcements concerning it be issued.

... And that it will not be long, probably sometime during the summer—when we can take the people of the city into our confidence—not that we do not want to take them into our confidence now, but I mean that we will mature those things to a point where they can be fully placed before the people, and we can show them in detail, department by department, just what the plan of action by this government is.

Mayor Mitchel was defeated for reelection partly through the pressures of the hostile Hearst newspapers, which supported his opponent. But when Mitchel was killed in an airplane accident on July 6, 1918, after he had lost his bid for reelection, newspapers poured out their affection and esteem for this man who had made "New York City a model of municipal efficiency."[19] Editorials in *The Sun* and the *New York Press* hailed Mitchel as a "professional city administrator." *The World* regarded Mitchel as "an executive of extraordinary ability, honesty, and fearlessness."

... He had had a brilliant civil career. ... Nothing that the voters of New York have done in a generation reflected less credit upon their intelligence than the wanton sacrifice of the most able city administrator that most of them had ever known. After the lapse of six months thousands of them have begun to realize what it means to New York to substitute a Hylan for a Mitchel, and it is impossible that the lesson will be forgotten. ... John Purroy Mitchel was an extraordinary able executive in spite of all the sneers and reproaches that a government by experts incurred.[20]

The Tribune noted: "For the small placating of public opinion in groups or classes he had no gift or patience.[21] The Class of 1899 of Columbia College wrote in memoriam that "the press has recorded in its newspaper columns the public achievements of John Purroy Mitchel and has paid unanimous and ardent tribute to his public services."[22]

Mayor Mitchel had acted as his own press secretary, for he had sought to make the media an external extension of his office, which would report factual happenings or act to mobilize and mold public opinion. To do this, in part, the mayor delivered major addresses that newspapers were required to print exactly. (He abhorred interpretation made by others and quotes taken out of context, and, where possible, he tried to prevent such reporting.)

Newspaper reporters covering City Hall deeply respected him. They did not get headline materials, but they did get unadulterated facts. There was no credibility gap in Mitchel's administration because he did not use the newspaper media to create an expurgated image of himself. Mayor Mitchel effectively and simply used the press to report the daily workings of his office.

Judge Hylan, who assumed office on January 1, 1918, had been elected in part because of the support of the Hearst newspapers. Harry Chandler, publisher of the Los Angeles *Times* and an enemy of Hearst, stated a possible reason why Hearst would back a Tammany man:

... People out in my state are worrying for fear [Hearst] is gunning now for the Presidency by proxy. ... They are keenly aware that he virtually made himself Mayor of New York by electing his own creature, Hylan, whom he could control ...

If cynics would say that Hearst was not so interested in placing able men in office as he was in electing men who would do his bidding, it should be noted to Hearst's credit that Hylan was honest. For all his many faux pas, he steered a straight course and never became involved in scandal.[23]

Politically, the relationship between Hearst and Hylan affected the Tammany machinery, for Hearst had become more Hylan's "boss" than the Tammany leader, Murphy.

For nineteen years Murphy had been forced to fight Hearst or to collaborate with him. He may have been hard put to tell which was worse. He personally detested the publisher, but he could never ignore him. In normal city politics, the Tammany leader had patronage claims which no dutiful Tammany mayor could refuse to honor.

With Hylan it was different. The mayor, who had grown annoyingly
vain because of his friendship with the publisher, did not show the
deference due Murphy as boss. It was no secret that Hearst was far
more Hylan's boss than Murphy was, and this was a humiliating
situation which Murphy was powerless to solve. So far, Hylan, who
had nominal control of city jobs and patronage, had appointed most
of the men Murphy wanted. But this was done with the understanding
that it was with the approval of Hearst. This placed Murphy in the
position of asking Hearst for favors which he should normally have
demanded of the mayor as his due. It also gave Hearst a ready weapon,
for if Murphy displeased him in any way, he could strike back at the boss
through Hylan.

In addition:

This was entirely apart from Hearst's financial help, always important
in an election, and the power of his press. Murphy was no more than
a sub-boss, and when he and Hearst elected Hylan for a second term
in 1921, it seemed that Murphy was in for four more years of sub-
bossism.[24]

. . .

His alliance with Hearst cost him the support of practically every
other newspaper in the city, though up to 1921 the circulation of
the Hearst papers was probably equal to that of all the rest. The
Hylan-Hearst partnership had considerable advantage for the Mayor's
Tammany backers, but it was at the same time, fraught with serious
menace because of the political instability of the powerful ambitions
of William Randolph Hearst.[25]

In spite of the fact that Hylan once said, "Mr. Hearst
never asks me for anything,"[26] he was doing things for Hearst
in return for his support. He quietly appointed Marion
Davies' father as a City Magistrate. (Miss Davies was Hearst's
well-known mistress.) When Marion Davies participated in a
New York show as a leading actress, the mayor sought to
make headlines in his comments.

Mayor Overwhelmed by Beauty and Story of "Knighthood Film."
    The acting of Miss Davies in the role of Princess Mary Tudor is
marvelous.[27]

Hylan publicly supported Hearst on all issues:

Mayor Hylan yesterday returned from a brief vacation spent at his birthplace in the Catskill Mountains. At the City Hall, he made public a letter written to William Randolph Hearst. The Mayor's letter follows:

Dear Mr. Hearst:

I read with great interest your answers to the questions profounded by Cornelius Vanderbilt, Jr., in his interview published last Sunday. It was a masterly presentation of your views of the subjects discussed. The questions which you answered are uppermost in the minds of the people of the nation.[28]

Only the *New York Journal* could publish the above.

Hylan's "devotion" for Hearst went to absurd lengths:

Louis Master, a Flushing realtor, put out a six-foot sign in front of his office reading "Do not read the Hearst newspapers." He was arrested by a Hylan policeman for "creating a disturbance."[29]

In return for his public devotion to Hearst, Hylan was successfully advertised by men from Hearst's able staff:

They were marvelously clever in the way they sold him, just as one might a soap. His picture appeared almost daily, usually in some act of kindness or fondling his grandchild, something of human interest.

On July 3, 1922, to cite one delicious example, there appeared in the *New York American,* a picture of a huge electric flag on City Hall, with an insert of the jovial-faced mayor. Below it one read: "This American flag, the largest in the world, has been erected on City Hall by Mayor Hylan. The light from this flag will shine out on the spot where Nathan Hale was hung by the British."

Frequently this publicity was in poor taste. Every place tried to imprint his name, such as on play streets.[30]

So publicized became Hylan, that a group of Republican reformers called the Citizens Union, offered "to speak for the independent voters of the city, and gathered up all the ills of seven lean years under the term Hylanism."[31]

It was reported that Hylan rose early and read the newspapers, and he often answered articles he had read in the newspapers. In a "Letter to the Editor" of *The New York World Tribune,* dated January 19, 1925, (see end of Chapter 3) the mayor wrote:

There is one statement in the series of articles on the public schools now appearing in the *Herald Tribune* which is so false and gives such an erroneous impression, that in fairness to your readers I believe you will want to carry this statement.

The mayor then responded to an "atrocious falsehood."

. . . The people are beginning to understand where the *Herald Tribune* is to be found upon questions of civic decency and progress and why it's to be found there.

A letter the mayor received from Thomas A. Farley, Democratic leader of the 14th Assembly District, was released to the papers:

. . . In common with other organization Democrats I am much amused by the anti-Democratic press trying to dictate to the Democratic party who it should nominate for mayor this fall. The fact that you are so personally obnoxious to these papers and those they represent is to your credit and cannot possibly prejudice you with a single organization Democrat of New York or of any honest fair-minded person.

While these papers like to dictate the Democratic nominees they never support them, and no matter what candidate may be nominated by the Democratic Party the same newspapers will be unanimously against them. . . .

If the press which is continuously attacking you desires to be really helpful to the New York taxpayer they would at least in some instances favor those improvements and policies which you and the Democratic Party have continuously advocated.[32]

On June 26, 1925, Mayor Hylan sent a letter to Chairman Pell of the Democratic State Committee noting an item that he had read in the newspapers.

It was very gratifying for me to read your statement in the newspapers. I think the great mass of the people feel that the government of city has been so administered that "New York City can hold up her head with any city in the world," as you say; and this notwithstanding the gross misrepresentation of the aims and purposes, the progress and achievements of the past seven and a half years which has been the daily diet fed to the people by the newspapers, the traction and financial backers which have had their plans of exploitation interfered with by a humane and honest city administration. . . .[33]

The men from Hearst's staff also helped the mayor promote his policies successfully. The mayor resorted to loaded and propagandized language, once even making use of ascribed status by quoting President Coolidge. He quoted from the newspapers to attack certain organizations. In a meeting of departments at City Hall on June 22, 1925, the mayor stated:

... There really isn't anything strange about the printing of the Citizen's Union gibberish—that political propaganda organization has a traction affiliation, and the greater part of the metropolitan newspapers are equally affiliated. And you may also count upon it that any fish story or long yarn of the Citizen's Union in an attempt to discredit the administration will be conspicuously displayed in such newspapers.[34]

The mayor castigated the papers and their allies for announcing the possibility that the five-cent subway fare might be increased. He released a statement to the press, heavy in loaded and propagandized language, the bulk of it published in the Hearst press.

My fight, and the fight of the people, regardless of party, is to maintain the five-cent fare and to give the people decent and adequate transit service. The fight of the increased-fare manipulators and their friends in newspaper and official circles is for the purpose of getting control of the city government so that they can also seize control of the new independent subway system and put over the increased fare billion dollar deal. [35]

A Hearst staff member helped Mayor Hylan write an autobiography to publicize his administration further (and to express his views on the press as well):

... Not surprising ... that many of our very best citizens positively refuse to assume the duties of citizenship insofar as public office is concerned. They are not willing that their good names shall be cartooned and lampooned; that their wives and children shall look into their faces and wonder if it is possible that an irresponsible mountebank can know more of the virtues of father than the wife and children around the hearthstone; that a snickering, sniveling snarl shall be lifted against them by a jaundiced eyed and nagging public who have been taught through the ribald and rasping satire of some smart chap, whose urge is the dignified but nonetheless virulent prescription of editors, which for lack of a better term is best described as editorial billingsgate, emanating from sources from which the public has a right to expect the best but gets the worst, that one of the vested rights of the press is to hold up in contempt any public official that may not square to its standard of measurement. So the heartless paragrapher and the phrase maker, who too frequently mistake sauce for sense and taunt for talent, proceed with their bombardment of words and the people, more or less as a jest, in answer throw up an embankment and have pop guns shoot votes at them. . . .[36]

Despite all his efforts to gain favorable publicity, the mayor did not receive much support from the press, except the Hearst papers, and he responded accordingly. The Mayor addressed the American Institute of Homeopathy at the Roosevelt Hotel with tirade.

The difficulty, however, we have had is to get before the people of the city the essential information which should be had of our public institutions that are supported by public money and dedicated to the public service. One reason for this unfortunate situation is that some newspapers and others to serve a partisan purpose conceal the facts about municipal progress and say things, particularly when a campaign is approaching, that are both untrue and absurd. . . .[37]

The mayor made his attitude toward the general press clear, once again, in an address delivered on the first anniversary of the New York City radio station WNYC.

Station WNYC is owned and controlled by the people of the City of New York. For the past year it has served many valuable purposes.

It has assisted the Police Department in the work of crime prevention and detection and has aided in bringing many lost persons back to their families.

And our people are getting the truth over the radio. Don't forget that the truth is the firmest bond of union yet devised and that it furnishes the most prominent basis for individual and collective happiness.

You know how persistently many of the newspapers misrepresent actual conditions in this city. They play the hurdy-gurdy of the traction corporations and echo the wind of the defamers of the city. They print every statement of every political noise-maker who may go through city departments with a fine-tooth comb, and, finding nothing, spins a long yarn, talks twaddle or deliberately misrepresents.[38]

Despite this antipathy towards the press, Mayor Hylan did give reporters freedom of access to City Hall. The mayor's remarks at a dinner reflected his basic attitude toward all reporters who were not Hearst employees.

It was the custom in years past to allow the freest possible latitude to all comers around Police Headquarters. The reputable newspaper men had to mingle with the space writers and free lancers, and, in fact, every person who came along and gave authorities the impression that he was connected in some way with an important publication in the community was given the greatest liberty and latitude around Police Headquarters.[39]

When Alfred E. Smith became governor, Hearst tried to make a deal with him to support Hylan's reelection bid against Jimmy Walker in 1925 in return for his support for Smith's candidacy for the presidency.

Governor Smith had the code. He knew what Hearst was offering to him. To his credit, he rejected it, doubtless feeling that it could not be depended on anyway. Smith's political fortunes had risen sharply since his first defiance of Hearst, and he was determined to finish the job. He saw to it that Tammany ditched Hylan and nominated the handsome, song-writing James J. Walker, Democratic leader in the state senate, for mayor. . . .[40]

Hylan entered the primary against Jimmy Walker with 25,000 dollars in campaign money from Hearst. The Hearst press, editorially and pictorially began dramatizing the sinister nature of Walker. (One cartoon depicted Walker as looking on approvingly as a dope peddler sold drugs to a child.) [41] Propaganda against Hearst was written by the other city newspapers and political groups. "Is William R. Hearst to be continued as the virtual ruler of the biggest city in the Western Hemisphere?" the Women's Democratic Union asked. The *Times* said of Hylan, "For him there is but one leader and boss, the Shepherd of St. Simeon."

The Hearst people drafted a letter to Senator Copeland, dated August 25, 1925, for the release in which Hylan indicated his determination to win the election:

I note that the traction newspapers confidently predict that Governor Alfred E. Smith is about to come here from Albany and throw his great mantle of political popularity around Candidate Walker and advise the people to vote for candidate Walker in the primary.

If it is true that the Governor proposes to openly ally himself with those who are trying to "jimmy" their way into the City Hall, then all I have to say is that we will have to meet that situation in the most direct and forceful manner possible. . . .[42]

A publicity pamphlet entitled the *ABC of Hylanism* was to strengthen the mayor's bid for renomination, purportedly to "show clearly what are the principles and doctrines which Mayor Hylan had put into practice." The booklet was prepared and presented by a group of "nonpartisan businessmen," which in reality meant Hearst.

I is for INTERESTS, the Wall Street gang and selfish capitalists who make millions out of public utilities. . . . They are moving heaven and earth now, through the traction-controlled newspapers, through their friends in political organizations; through lying, falsehood, and every influence, to nominate their own candidates. . . .

K is for KNOCKS you ofttimes hear. . . . But for the mayor every knock is a boost. . . . You'll find all their knocks in the "Subway Sun." . . .[43]

R is for RADIO and RECREATION. It was the Hylan administration, which established the Municipal Radio Station WNYC, which keeps the people of New York informed about the affairs of their city government, and which provides nightly programs for their instruction and entertainment. . . .   H
A Word of Five letters meaning Progress — H Y L A N
                                        L
                                        A
                                        N

Mayor Hylan lost the primary, and Hearst went on to[44] support Jimmy Walker. "It seems that the people don't want me after all I have done for them," was Hylan's swan song. And Hearst's *American* said Hylan "was the victim of a plot laid in the inner councils of Wall Street."[45] Mayor Hylan denounced those newspapers who had not been writing news copy and molding public opinion as he and Hearst had wanted it.

To summarize, Hylan had yielded the responsibility of administering his publicity in the papers to members of the

Hearst newspaper staff. Accordingly, the mayor continuously
attacked reporters, other than Hearst employees, and stooped
to irresponsible pejorative, and inflammatory remarks. His
publicity had been conducted neither in decorum nor
dignity but reflected the Hearst style of irresponsible
"yellow journalism." Hylan did this because he had needed
the direct support of William Randolph Hearst to gain the
office of mayor of New York City. And if there were any
loyalty between Hearst and Hylan it was politically motivated,
for Hearst dropped Judge Hylan when there was "no longer
any percentage of the cut."[46] Certainly no sense of personal
intimacy or respect prevailed between the two men.

APPENDIX

Mayor Hylan's "Letter to the Editor,"
New York Herald-Tribune, January 19, 1925

Dear Sir:
    There is one statement in the series of articles on the public schools
now appearing in the *Herald-Tribune,* which is so absolutely false and
gives such an erroneous impression, that, in fairness to your readers, I
believe you will want to carry this statement.
    In alleging existing elementary school congestion, the article states
that this was created "because of the crowded conditions brought about
by Mayor Hylan's long delay in building schools." This is an atrocious
falsehood.
    There has not been a day's delay in the building of public schools
since this administration took office. The World War was in progress
the first year of our administration, 1918. The War Industries Board
had ordered the suspension of all non-war construction. This affected
the public schools. In the early part of 1918, I wrote to the chairman
of the Priorities Committee of the War Industries Board stating, among
other things:
    I regret to be obliged to appeal to you in the matter of the construc-
tion of new elementary school buildings in the City of New York. The
people of the city are entitled to and must have sufficient schools to
properly house the children and give them an elementary education.
The people of New York are doing their part in aiding the government
in its great war work and we hope that your board will recognize the
necessity for releasing material to enable the Board of Education to
proceed with the buildings necessary for giving our children the required
elementary schooling.

My request was not granted and the embargo on building materials was not lifted until some time in the spring of 1919. Do you charge this administration with a failure to proceed with public school construction during the period of the Embargo when the United States Government would not permit such construction?

You do not charge the administration which preceded without delay. Yet that administration practically built no new public schools. To make certain that none would be built in the immediate future, it caused the Pay-As-You-Go-Law to be enacted and which went into full effect when we took office. If we had not secured a prompt amendment of this law, no new public schools would have been built. The conditions of neglect extending over a period of twenty years would have reached such a crisis as to make an early and adequate improvement a virtual impossibility. Why do you not tell that had there been no neglect to construct adequate school accommodation during the past twenty years, the people of this city would have been saved almost half the cost of the public school appropriations which we have been obliged to make to remedy that neglect.

After charging the Hylan administration with neglect to build new public schools you then inadvertently admit that public school construction has been going on. You state, "Mayor Hylan believes in building huge schools of impressive appearance despite his frequent references to 'the little red schoolhouse up-house up-State' where he received his education."

New York City with its school growing population of more than a million children needs huge schools. Even the *Herald-Tribune* will acknowledge that. Progress demands it. The little red schoolhouse has its place but certainly not in the world's greatest city. Adequate school accommodations are a vital necessity to the welfare of the City of New York. A decent regard for the hopes and aspirations of parents to secure sound education for their children demand them. The very life of this nation is in the last analysis dependent in large measure upon them.

Yet the picture of large and ornate school buildings erected by this administration and which if placed side by side would reach from the Battery to 135th Street seems to disturb you.

The *Herald-Tribune* heartily endorses President Coolidge. Does it endorse this statement of his: "The old one-room country school, such as I attended, ought to give way to the consolidated school with a modern building and an adequate teaching force commensurate with the best advantages that are provided for our urban population."

This administration endorses that declaration. As evidence of it we have in addition to the new public school buildings already opened 70 or more structures in course of completion. It is anticipated that

53 of them will be ready for the children at the opening of the fall school term this year. When the 70 new buildings, with their seating capacity of 125,773, are completely constructed every child attending elementary schools in this city will be provided with a seat on regular schedule. With the possible exception of one borough all of the high school pupils will likewise be on regular schedule. And all this will be done without any resort to the Gary System, upon which the parents of this city twice passed judgment.

This administration has refused to surrender to the traction and public utility corporations. We have been hounded by these disappointed self-seekers from the first day we entered office. We have refused to surrender to the Rockefeller-Gary educational coterie. For this we have been hounded. We have refused to permit the gambling and underworld interests to run this city at the sacrifice of young manhood and young womanhood and to the detriment of legitimate business enterprises whose very existence depends upon a clean city, well administered.

The people are beginning to understand where the *Herald-Tribune* is to be found upon questions of civic decency and progress and why it is to be found there.

Very truly yours,

John F. Hylan
Mayor

FOUR

JAMES J. WALKER

Jimmy Walker had been a New York State senator when Governor Smith had maneuvered to have Tammany Hall nominate him to run against Mayor Hylan in the summer of 1925. Walker won the election by a plurality of 402,123, Tammany's first unequivocal victory since 1902 when Mayor Van Wyck had lost. Rarely had a new mayoral administration begun with such broad public support. "Jimmy," served as mayor from 1926 to 1932. Both his personal and public life were colorful, grandiose, and dramatic. He was loved and respected by the newspapermen and others more as a "great guy" to be with than as a political figure.

During one of his visits to France, the Paris edition of the *Herald-Tribune* described Mayor Walker in the following manner:

Of Mayor Walker it may be said that he represents in a preeminent degree American commonsense, cleverness, alertness, adaptability and good humor.[1]

Sophie Tucker once said about Mayor Walker,

Wherever he went, you would have thought he was a combination of General Grant and Mark Twain and the United States Supreme Court. There's no question about it. . . .[2]

Republican newspapers published editorials wishing the bright young Walker the best of luck and intimating that he might be a success despite the taint of Tammany. Even William Randolph Hearst's "paper dynasty," the *American,* the *Journal,* and the *Mirror* had offered a few congratulations.

The press of the city seemed pleased with Walker's election. After he took office in January 1926, headlines expressed wonder at the new spirit of harmony and peace and expeditiousness which he had brought to City Hall. The *New York Times,* in an editorial, stated:

At the beginning of Mayor Walker's fourth week in office the good people of New York still find themselves sitting up with a shock and wondering what queer city it is that figures so largely in the morning papers. It is a city whose mayor has developed the most extraordinary habits and practices. When he wants to discuss matters affecting the commercial future of the part of New York, he gets in touch with the Chamber of Commerce. When he decides to look into transit matters, he makes an appointment with the Transit Commission. When he is interested in streets and traffic, he establishes communication with the Merchants' Association. The climax was attained when Mayor Walker, desiring to ascertain what might be done to improve the subway service by enlarging three platforms at local I.R.T. stations, actually invited representatives of the I.R.T. to meet him in conference. What this extraordinary public official will do next is not to be predicted.[3]

Walker appointed as his Assistant to the Mayor, Charles F. Kerrigan, a former newspaper man on the *New York World.* Kerrigan served Mayor Walker as a "technique and tools" man, but the mayor conducted all of his press relations. The reporters liked him; they served him and they protected him whenever they could.

Mayor Walker had many special friends among the newspaper people including Paul Block, proprietor of the *Newark News,* the *Toledo Blade,* and the *Brooklyn Standard Union,* Edward McClean, publisher of the *Washington Post.* He also was friends with Damon Runyon, Jack Lait, Heywood Broun, Ring Lardner, Sid Mercer, Stanley Walker, Bob Ripley, Irving Cobb, and many others. The usual meeting spot was Toots Shor's restaurant.

When Walker had been in the New York State Senate, most of the Albany correspondents became his fast friends, for he never lied to them.

Some editors of the New York press thought Walker was a charming "wastrel." They admitted, however, that he got things done at Albany and, as a speaker, had become a brilliant star. Other editors, especially the well-known Bayard Swope of the *Morning World,* championed Walker's career. Publisher Paul Block of the *Brooklyn Standard Union* was known to have given the Mayor a fur-lined topcoat, as well as to have established a fund—beneficence—for him for "additional personal" living expenses.

The author of *Beau James,* Gene Fowler, was the managing editor of the Hearst's *New York American.* Many of the *American* staff were loyal friends and admirers of Walker, at the very time that Hearst ordered his newspaper to attack the mayor during the 1925 primary campaign of Hylan against Walker. The Albany correspondent, Robert Watson, had a real affection for Walker. Damon Runyon and others in the sports department liked him immensely.

Mayor Walker bantered with and cajoled the press, which made them partners of a sort in a political game. During Marshal Petain's visit to City Hall, the Mayor had presented him with a medal, but the mayor had difficulty pinning it on. The Mayor drew back and said, "Marshall, I see that you have been reading our newspapers, but you have been misinformed. It was unnecessary for you to appear before us today in a bullet-proof vest."[4]

As an example of how the press tended to protect the mayor, Paul Crowell, an extraordinarily capable *Times* reporter, stumbled on the fact that New York was not keeping up on its payments for municipal supplies. It was something he had dug out of the *City Record.* Further investigation established that the city was financially wobbly and that it was desperately trying to raise $60,000,000 to tide it over a bad period. When publisher Adolph Ochs of the *Times* read Crowell's story he was gravely concerned. "Mr. Crowell," he said, "shouldn't you let Mayor Walker know we have the facts? If we just run the story without some comment from him, it will embarrass the city and damage its credit."

Crowell knew Walker's charm. "I wouldn't talk to the Mayor," he told the publisher. "He will talk us out of the story."[5] Ochs phoned the Mayor. Crowell was right. Walker talked the *Times* out of running the story on the ground that its publication would make it impossible for the city to borrow the $60,000,000. Three weeks later, and long before the Seabury investigations were to uncover further financial difficulties for the city and the Mayor, the story broke in all the newspapers. Crowell was unhappy; he had been deprived of an exclusive story which he had uncovered. Ochs still felt he had acted for the common good; his concept of his job was that of a publisher who assumed social responsibility for himself and his profession.

The reporters also protected Mayor Walker by avoiding any mention in print of the rift between the mayor and Mrs. Walker.

It was not exactly a secret that newspapermen knew of the rift between the Walkers. . . O'Connor knew about it, as did Kaufman and Winchell. At this time, Winchell, although employed by Bernarr Macfadden's *Graphic,* was contributing anonymously to the *Telegraph*'s famous old column "Beau Broadway." We frequently received letters denouncing us for having a Winchell "imitator" on our staff. And sometimes Winchell's anonymous scooped his regular column in the *Graphic.*

It was Winchell's self-imposed policy, no matter how hot the news, never to mention the indiscretions of any man or woman unless one or both parties were contemplating an appearance in the divorce court. Indeed that was the general practice among newspapermen of that day.

The reporters tried to protect him [Walker] from himself, for he took almost no precaution to conceal his way of living. The Park Row writers did not wish to penalize the man for his lack of hypocrisy, when all around him there were public figures who posed in piety and righteousness but cavorted behind the doors of their secret harems.[6]

Mayor Walker was all human—he drank, he danced, he had failings—he knew it, he was fun, and he was bright. There was even some fear that he might give up his happy ways.

Among those friendly viewers of alarm are certain gentlemen of the press who cover the City Hall. Almost unanimously his ardent sup-porters, they nevertheless urge upon him a great deal more promptness and regularity. When he does not arrive at his office until noon, having been dancing until dawn at some night club, they obligingly and protest-ingly omit mentioning that fact in their papers.[7]

Reporters could always call the Mayor at home, where no one served as an intermediary. But, though the reporters had a sense of camaraderie for Walker, they did not hesitate to chastise him and he them. Walker's absences from City Hall were commented upon by the newspapers for example. The *New York Herald-Tribune* pointed out that Mayor Walker had taken several vacations during his first two years in office. A front-page story in the Sunday edition of the *New York Times* on March 14, 1928 asked the following: "Who, if anybody at the present moment, is the acting mayor of New York?" The story went on to say that the Mayor was out of town, the President of the Board of Aldermen, Joseph V. McKee, was at Palm Beach where his wife was recuperating from an illness, and the Vice-Chairman of the Board, Charles A. McManus, was also in the South.[8]

Two days after Walker's acceptance to run for a second term, a major newspaper carried an editorial bearing the head, "The Mayor He Might Be". . . .

Men are often judged by the wrong qualities. . . . If, for example, the people of this city were asked to sum up the official character of Mayor Walker, nine out of ten of them would dwell upon his great personal charm, his talent for friendship, his broad sympathies embrac-ing all sorts and conditions of men, his ready wit, his brilliance as a speaker at every kind of gathering or function, his skill as a politician, his gift for winning support from the most unlikely quarters.

Mr. Walker has a singularly alert intelligence. He is quick not only in epigram and repartee, but in grasp of the essentials of a governmental problem laid before him.[9]

On a few occasions Walker gave voice to a resentment against the press that was rare in his earlier mayoral career. His belief had always been that criticism of public men was inevitable and useless to combat. Responding to the sting of newspaper disapprobation, he commented:

> . . . It is only bad news that is good news for a newspaper. They can sell nothing but knocks. At least they seem to think so.[10]

During the outbreak of gang warfare in New York in 1931 two children were shot. Soon after the crime was committed, a reporter from a New York newspaper telephoned the mayor at his apartment asking, "How did Walker feel about children being shot down?" The Mayor was so livid at the stupidity of the question that he could not speak coherently. A friend who was with him at the time had to call the newspaper back to reply to the question.

Before taking office Walker had told his friends that he was not going to be a "signboard."[11] This was intended to mean that His Honor, with friends in every kind of profession, was not going to allow himself to be used by motion-picture stars, golf champions, evangelists, pugilists, and other transient personages who wanted to be photographed with him on the steps of City Hall. He either soon forgot this resolution or his ability to say "no" failed him.

Mayor Walker's typical method of attacking the park, hospital, or subway problem was to summon one of his limousines and fill another with cameramen, so that the pictorial tabloid patrons might see the hard-working mayor in action.

The endless stream of visiting mayors, governors, other high officials, leading members of Congress and the Cabinet, and eminent representatives of science and the arts to City Hall all found themselves at one point or another during their trip being photographed with the Mayor and then appearing in every paper in New York and in their home territory. Thus he might have been presiding over a meeting at the Board of Estimate, when an aide would slip up to him and whisper that the Irish world's champion hockey players or a young lady representing the first sap of Vermont maple trees had arrived in City Hall. The mayor would pass the gavel to the President of the Board of Aldermen, Joseph V. McKee, and disappear. He would go out on the steps of City Hall and the photographers would begin clicking their cameras.

His Honor smiles holding up the hockey stick, syrup . . . as the case may be. The stills drop back to reload. The "movies" rattle into place. The mayor swings the stick, tilts the can or otherwise gestures appropriately. Then a second round of stills; then a parting shot for the movies; and, five minutes having elapsed, the mayor slips unobtrusively into his seat. . . .[12]

Walker's inauguration was the first to be broadcast. Concerning his successful use of the radio, John Carlisle of the Columbia Broadcasting Company noted that "Mayor Walker's voice is probably one of the most colorful voices we have ever observed in the study of radio voices. It is a free voice, as ready and apt in the sounding of sentences as its possessor is in the framing of them."[13]

Within a few years of his arrival in Albany, Walker had become a popular speaker, and the New York City reporters considered him good enough copy to devote considerable space to his remarks.

One day Senator Walker began to talk to a major audience with an alarming confession that brought the house down.

He said that he had been asked to prepare his speech in advance, and he had done so. But the speech he had dictated to the stenographer he had given to the press agent of the hotel where he was to speak, and he had then lost his own copy.[14]

Mayor Walker actually had no speech writer. He always spoke extemporaneously. His words had the backing of his personality, and he kept his audience entertained. He never used notes, although he had been known to make them.

The mayor once had asked his publishing friend, Paul Block, to listen to a speech he had prepared for the Lindbergh reception. Block made several changes, welcomed by Walker. However, when the day came to deliver the address, Walker delivered the best extemporaneous address he had ever made, never bothering with the prepared speech.

In a newspaper interview published in 1929, Walker indicated his attitude toward speech-writing.

One of the things I have observed most often is the bored look of the crowd when the speaker begins to praise the guest of honor. A man

can't be human and measure up to this eulogy. When such a speaker
unfurls his flag, you can feel the thermometer drop. If a man has
accomplished something worthwhile, we like to be told about it, but
in a plain way—the plainer the more convincing. We believe that the
speaker means what he is saying. I have attended hundreds of dinners
in the last four years, and a man who sits at the speaker's table night
after night gets to understand the faces before him. They are mighty
interesting to watch. When a speaker takes the wrong track, or the
right one, it is easy to see the effect. I sometimes wonder if the man
speaking ever looks at the audience. Evidently not, or he could read
the signs better.[15]

Mayor Walker did not appoint a press secretary to schedule
his appointments or to act as a buffer, for he took charge of
things himself. He never delegated responsibility for over-
seeing a publicity project but controlled it himself. Several
examples demonstrate this. The Charles A. Lindbergh
reception had aroused the excitement of the people of New
York City. Elaborate arrangements at City Hall for the
reception and the handling of the crowds had created a
tension that had caused several flareups. One conflict occurred
between Hector Fuller, Walker's master of ceremonies at
greeting parties, and the radio men. Fuller had been assigned
the task of introducing the principal and reading the honor
scroll, and Tommy Cowan, an announcer for the municipal
station, was to broadcast the ceremonies for both WNYC and
the national hook-up.

At the last moment while Walker was out on the grandstand awaiting the
arrival of the guest of honor, Fuller announced that he would assume
charge of the broadcasting functions as well. The officials of the radio
chains objected, and the ensuing bitter dispute reached the ears of
Walker. He assumed his characteristic quizzical expression and inquired
of Cowan, who was standing by uncertain what to do: "Have you
suddenly grown dumb?"

"No, Your Honor," replied Cowan.

"Well, your reply convinces me," said Walker, and then taking
Fuller by the hand, began instructing him:

"Now, Hector," he said, as Fuller, an ultra-dignified gentleman,
listened stiffly. "Everybody in the world knows that Lindbergh is coming
here this morning and that I've appointed you Master of Ceremonies.
There's a little red dais up there about thirty-five feet from here, where

you will announce to me that Colonel Lindbergh has arrived. Of course, I'll know it myself, for there'll be plenty of cheering to indicate it. But officially speaking, he will not be here until you tell me, thirty-five feet ahead of these microphones."[16]

A few days later at a Lindbergh dinner the mayor again took control. The dinner was to have been broadcast through a national network, and last-minute changes in the wiring were found necessary. Walker had suspected that something was wrong, and instead of delegating the inquiry to someone else, excused himself and left the dais. "What is the matter?" the mayor asked the chief announcer of WNYC, Tommy Cowan. As Cowan began to search for an excuse, he cut him short with, "Come on. Let's have it. You don't have to kid me." The mayor grinned and calmly asked Cowan how long it would take to repair the wires. He was told about ten minutes. "I guess I can stall them for fifteen minutes. Go ahead and fix it. And remember, don't lose your head, and you won't lose your job."[17]

Walker attracted his usual amount of notice during his European trips, and his personality and repartee became as popular with the foreign press as with newsmen in the United States.

One individual that equalled Walker in his publicity techniques was Benito Mussolini, *Il Duce*. Once after Mayor Walker had an interview with Mussolini in Rome, the Italian leader pressed several buttons, and a cameraman and an electrician bearing spotlights entered. Mussolini personally helped to place the apparatus in the best position and super-intended the filming of a newsreel of himself and the Mayor, as well as of the other visitors. Mussolini then issued a public statement:

Mayor Walker is young, not only in appearance but also in spirit. He is a man of great talent, an idealist, and a practical man at the same time. Therefore, he is highly fitted to govern the great metropolis where millions of Italians live and whom the New York Mayor has praised, saying they were upright, hard-working, and obedient to American laws. I believe his journey through Italy will be instrumental in furthering that better reciprocal knowledge of our two peoples, which is the basis of true and lasting friendship between them.[18]

In Berlin the first question newspapermen directed to him was "What do you think of Berlin?" And his quick-witted reply was "That's not so important as what Berlin thinks of me." When asked why he said that, the jovial mayor retorted, "Because I haven't seen anything of Berlin and you have seen all of me." And at a luncheon tendered by the Anglo-American Press Club in Paris he was introduced as "God's gift to newspapermen." He addressed the luncheon guests as "Distinguished visitors and fellow refugees from the Eighteenth Amendment." (The Eighteenth constitutional amendment prohibited the sale of alcoholic beverages.)

When Walker was in London, the newspapermen began writing the mass of reports that filled the British newspapers during his stay in Europe. One journalist wrote an account of the Mayor's personality. Evidently thinking it might be too frank, the journalist asked Walker to read it first.

He is a rare Mayor; a Mayor of the type not often seen in this country. He stays up so late that he is sometimes called the "night Mayor"; but he shows that it is possible to sleep until midday and still retain a reputation for hustling; that it is possible to be a jester and still keep his dignity, and to wear canary-colored socks without inciting ridicule. He once wrote a popular sentimental song, but his reputation as a business man has not suffered. He is a humorist, but he is also a humanist. He takes his work seriously, but he does not take himself too seriously.

Walker responded: "It's O. K. with me."[19]

Another satirical Walker comment at the luncheon delighted the newspapermen.

You know, it's great to have newspapermen pay for your lunch, but I knew it could never be done until there were at least a hundred or two of them to do it.

After the mayor had finished his address, the newspaper reporters gathered round the piano with him singing the songs of "Old New York." The Paris edition of the *Herald* summed up the Parisians' interest in the Mayor in a report published the second day of his stay:

Mayor Walker's arrival yesterday was hailed with a shower of eulogies
in the Press, but his political activities and administrative abilities
received second place in the description of his personality. . . . The
Mayor is compared to Lindbergh, but in the opinion of some of the
French writers he goes on better than the young hero of the Atlantic,
for he loves a good glass of wine.[20]

Some of Mayor Walker's press activities were staged. On
one of his trips to Europe during his administration, he was
to leave at night. As photographic equipment in those days
did not compensate well for darkness, on the day of the
departure, when the mayor was invited to a luncheon on the
boat, they pretended that this coming aboard at noon was
the actual start of the trip. On hand were a squad of police
and detectives and at least 50 photographers taking "stills."
Up on the boat-deck the photographers asked the Mayor and
Mrs. Walker to wave their hands as if they were actually
departing.

On his London tour, one newspaperman was inspired to
ask Walker why he was always late.

"Who says I am always late?" the mayor inquired.

"The clock does," he was told.

"Well now," he replied, "did you ever know a clock that could tell
the truth? Did you ever know two clocks that could tell the same lie
together? No, sir. You can't rely on a clock, and anyway, it isn't the
fellow who arrives on time according to the clock who gets things done
right. It's the fellow who fixes the things right when he does arrive. The
fact really is, I find people so interesting I simply can't treat them as
clocks and make a face about the time I should be leaving them.
Besides, the clock and I don't start the day together. I sleep and the
clock doesn't."[21]

Some of the articles in the European press were greatly
exaggerated and magnified. After his meeting with Mussolini,
whom Mayor Walker considered one of the great men of his
time, he remarked, "I don't believe it would be good form for
me to repeat what he said, especially since, when he wanted to
be quoted, he has his own press bureau through which he
gives out what he wants to say."[22]

Mayor Walker was sensitive to the problems of ethnic

groups of the city. On one occasion, a number of elderly
Jewish men, led by rabbis, paraded down Broadway to City
Hall from East New York to protest the massacre of Jews by
Arabs in Palestine. A Jewish journalist led the way for them
to meet the mayor, who had feared complications with politicians in Washington if he did meet them. "I was warned not
to receive these men. Everyone advised me against it for fear
-of Washington complications but I will see them. Bring them
all in!" He also endeared himself to the Jews and their ethnic
press further when he climbed out of a sick bed to attend a
protest meeting in Madison Square Garden.[23]

Charges had begun to accumulate asserting that Mayor
Walker had failed to administer the city governments, had
appointed unworthy officials, and had ignored widespread
corruption. In addition, there appeared to be damaging
evidence against Mayor Walker with regard to his finances and
financial dealings.

The mayor responded in a speech by stating that any
reports of corruption should have been disclosed long ago by
the press if they were doing their job. Heywood Broun,
Broadway columnist, said in a facetious statement,

In other words, the press has held out on James Joseph Walker.
Apparently no reporter took the trouble to tell the mayor the facts of
life in a great city. Somebody should blurt out to him the news that
there is no Santa Claus within the ranks of Tammany. At least, only
for a very restricted set of good little boys and girls.[24]

Judge Seabury was appointed by Governor Franklin Delano
Roosevelt to head an investigatory team, and the accounts of
Walker and many other public officials were subpoenaed.
When Judge Seabury put Mayor Walker on the witness stand
in the county courthouse, it was the major news of the day.
The *New York Times* played up the story, printing four
columns on page 1 plus several pages more of text and reactions
inside. The "smaller" headlines reported on the front page
included such items as a pitched battle between the Nazis and
Communists in the Prussian Diet Hall and President Hoover's
campaign for renomination.

Judge Seabury questioned Mayor Walker for two days, May 25 and 26, 1932. What Judge Seabury undertook to investigate resulted in three investigations within the City of New York of the magistrates' courts, the office of the district attorney, and the affairs of the entire City of New York. These full-scale inquiries culminated in the resignation of Mayor Walker and led to the fusion government of Mayor LaGuardia.

Seabury's investigation lasted two years. Seabury's view toward his frank line of attack during these two years was expressed by:

The public will not be aroused to an awareness of conditions . . . through a series of graphs, charts, and reports. We must divorce this investigation, as far as is possible, from legalistic machinery. There is more eloquence in the testimony of an illiterate witness . . . than in the greatest sermon, editorial or address ever written. Where preachers, editors, and lawyers have failed in arousing the public to a consciousness of unjust conditions, these simple, unlearned witnesses will succeed.[25]

The *New York Times* in an editorial wrote:

Till now nothing has come from the City Hall to indicate that Mr. Walker is aware of the discredit brought by his associates and subordinates upon his own record. When so many cracks show in the structure there is lowered resistance to stress. The hour has come for the Mayor to summon both the demolition and reconstruction crews. It is not too late for Mr. Walker, who has in no personal way been even slightly connected with any of these scandals, to voice the indignation of the community which has twice elected him. A Republican investigation is both inevitable and desirable, however his own chances of reelection are shown to be affected by what is happening here.[26]

Walker had been loyal to the incompetents in City Hall. In addition to appointing questionable magistrates, Walker had also appointed former Mayor Hylan to be judge of the children's court in Queens. When asked why he had appointed a man who had impugned his character, Walker told the reporter that the "appointment of Judge Hylan means the children now can be tried by their peer."

What happened in New York City was closely observed by Democratic Governor Roosevelt. Alfred E. Smith, when he was governor, had told Walker before the 1928 presidential convention that a scandal involving the mayor could affect a candidate from New York running for President. It could definitely cause the defeat of the present governor, for the governor needed the cooperation of Tammany Hall, the mayor, and the New York City independent voters.

As the investigation proceeded, Mayor Walker appealed through the news media and radio to the citizens to send him any information of petty graft. He pledged a cleanup of misdemeanors that might result from the day-to-day activities of 140,000 city employees. Judge Seabury also was as much aware of the power of publicity and the press as any politician. He was learning how to make headlines for the afternoon papers and at the same time leave a promise for the morning papers. The news stories were presented as scandal for the readers of the *New York Daily News* and as sociology for readers of the *New York Times.*

Congressman LaGuardia, whose accusations of graft and corruption in his unsuccessful campaign for mayor against incumbent Walker the previous fall, called Walker's plea "a joke." LaGuardia said:

How does he get away with it? Had I been elected, I would have cleaned out every city department myself. I would have removed every Tammany commissioner. The mere fact that the mayor publicly states that there is petty graft is proof that the commissioners of the departments know there is. What chance has a poor pushcart peddler when a demand is made on him to pay his tribute? What chance has the plumber who cannot get a license unless he sees someone? And so it goes all down the line.[27]

During the two days Walker was on the stand, he elaborated on the Tammany line that the investigation was not authorized and that New York City was being hurt. "This investigation has done much to undermine the value of New York securities and has done much to make it difficult to market them." Seabury, however, continued to examine Walker's financial records. The judge asked Walker to explain how he had received nearly a quarter of a million dollars over a two-year period from a joint brokerage account with Paul Block, his intimate friend and publisher of the *Brooklyn Standard Union.* Paul Block also sometimes acted for Hearst in buying up daily papers.

Walker concluded his last comment on the stand by alluding to the possibility that Seabury was hoping to run for political office. "I hope with the close of the two national conventions in Chicago we will be through with some of the politics."

Late in the afternoon of May 25, 1932, the mayor left the stand. "The cheering from the Tammany adherents," Raymond Daniell reported in the *New York Times,* "was just as strong as it had been when he came to court."[28] The long day was neatly summed up by Doris Fleeson in one lead sentence in the *New York Daily News:* "Mayor James J. Walker fought with rapier-like wit against the ponderous legal attack leveled at him by Samuel Seabury."[29] The *New York Times* headline read "Tammany Pleased by Walker Showing. Friends Told He Came Off Better Than Even Against Seabury in his Two Days on Stand."[30]

By the beginning of June 1932, Seabury felt the time had come to bring charges before Governor Roosevelt for the removal of Walker as Mayor of New York. But the Democratic presidential nominating convention was only weeks away, and both the Governor and the committee counsel would only allow their favorite newspapers to get stories. Neither took any step that might appear politically motivated, for, as the *New York Times* of June 3, 1932 stated, "To act on his own initiative now, the Governor's advisers have told him, would be to run the risk of being accused of political opportunism. The political effect of Mayor Walker's case on Governor Roosevelt's chances of winning his party's nomination for President cannot be minimized. Failure to act decisively if charges are filed with him might be interpreted as bowing to Tammany Hall, while precipitate action would alienate the local organization and cast doubt on Mr. Roosevelt's ability to carry his own state."[31]

After further hearings before the Governor and the State Legislature in Albany, Jimmy Walker resigned as Mayor of New York City. When Walker resigned Walter T. Brown, chief of the Albany Bureau of the Associated Press in 1932, wrote author Gene Fowler:

When Walker quit, I thought he made a mistake, as by that time Roosevelt had the presidency in the bag and couldn't lose. Walker could have been reelected on an exoneration platform. In 1941, after I entered the Army, I visited President Roosevelt at the White House. I asked him point-blank if he would have fired Walker. He said he did not believe the Seabury evidence justified it. He agreed with me that the political impossible has been lost in the inexorable shift of voters. Roosevelt always liked Walker but wouldn't trust his fluid emotions.[32]

After the resignation a sympathetic reporter said to the ex-Mayor, "Everyone is for you, Jim. All the world loves a lover."

"You are mistaken," Walker replied. "What the world loves is a winner."[33]

A factor which had contributed to Walker's resignation was that, as the case progressed, he became more acutely conscious of antagonisms that had been stirred up against him in many quarters. The newspapers particularly had become hostile. They made statements which exceeded even the journalistic license prevailing during election campaigns. To those familiar with the proceedings at the various hearings before the Committee and the Governor, the reports in the newspapers were surprising in the incorrect impression they often conveyed. Walker had not known such implacable, cruel offensive criticism before.

Counsel Walker was to retort:

Mr. Seabury is now a politician and I am not. He is a political boss and I am out of politics. So I have to make some allowance for the fact that, as a political boss, he must be expected to make statements for political campaign purposes. There never was a statement made by Mr. Seabury under circumstances that would permit the answer to go along with the charge at the same time. I've had a good deal of experience with that. He is still using me to get into the papers. His old style is innuendo and half-truth and misrepresentation.[34]

After several years of enforced retirement on the Riviera and elsewhere in Europe, ex-Mayor Walker was appointed by Mayor LaGuardia to a post as assistant counsel to the State Transit Commission. Citizen Seabury was still attacking and denounced the appointment. He said "the real aim of the appointment was that it came within two weeks of Walker's pension deadline from the City of New York."[35]

There are perhaps few things that please humans as much as recognizing that a very important man, whether his stature is one of position or wealth, lives as a mortal human being. Walker gave us that recognizance. He lived with the freedom of the ordinary individual, and in his excitement and enjoyment of life, he allowed "his press" to portray it fully. The American public has always set a code of behavior for such an individual, and even if it admires deviations from it, it neither tolerates them nor accepts them coolly. If there was caution, it was used by the journalists who were his friends.

It is hazardous for a high public official to make a world of his own and then govern himself by his own laws in full public view.

The last reception that Walker attended was shortly before his resignation. A private dinner was given to Captain Mollison, the aviator who had made the transatlantic solo flight from east to west. Walker, who had just returned from a hearing in Albany, came in unofficially. He was faced with a crisis in his personal-political life, and circumstances were bearing down upon him with inexorably destructive pressure, but he remained his usual gay self. His impromptu remarks brought warmth and laughter. "These are the days of reverses, Captain. I should receive you but you are receiving me. I should be pinning a medal on you but they are also trying to pin a medal on me."

A day after Walker's resignation, the *New York Times* published this dispatch from its German correspondent:

Berlin, Sept. 2—Comment here on James J. Walker's resignation testified to the impression he made on the popular imagination on his

two visits to Berlin, in 1927 and 1931, as an unconventional "Lord
Mayor" of the American metropolis. The *Vossiche Zeitung* runs nearly
two columns captioned "Jimmie" in which it dwells on his charm,
elegance, ready humor, pointed wit, gayety, and optimism.

With Walker a new type of Mayor, before unknown, came on the
political scene in the United States and after seven years' administration
it is difficult to think of him out of public life. New York without him
does not seem the same New York that so readily wins the hearts of
all foreign visitors going there without any prejudice or blinkers.[36]

Walker's publicity spanned cities, states, nations. He was
so well known throughout the country that during his administration City Hall received dozens of letters each day from
school children in every state asking "Jimmie Walker" to
please send them information either about himself or his city.

In general Mayor Walker's personality commanded publicity. He didn't have to go out of his way to "manufacture"
it. The people were more interested in Walker's charisma
than in his policies. That was the sort of newsmaking he
generated. When he became serious in an address or discussing a city policy, he felt out of character.

James V. McKee, President of the Board of Aldermen,
automatically became Acting Mayor upon the resignation of
Mayor Walker and served for four months. During the political campaign of October 1933, it was said about McKee that
"nothing can make him talk at a press interview when he's
made up his mind not to." Charles Keegan, a former police
commissioner, who later became a city councilman from the
Bronx, acted as McKee's press secretary. Since there was no
press secretary at this time, Keegan was officially "assistant to
the mayor." His responsibilities were minimal and little is
recalled about him.[37]

Tammany boss John F. Curry picked John P. O'Brien,
former surrogate of New York County, to run in the special
election held in November 1932. He won the election but
has become one of the most forgotten mayors in New York
City history. O'Brien, according to veteran newsman

Emanuel Perlmutter, was a caricature of the old clubhouse politician. Perlmutter recalled that Paul Crowell, one of the leading City Hall reporters and a *Times* man, asked Mayor O'Brien who was going to be his new police commissioner. O'Brien answered, "they haven't told me yet."[38]

O'Brien had no press secretary, and Mr. Perlmutter could remember that it was possible to telephone and immediately speak to the mayor.

Some minister out in Bensonhurst, Brooklyn had complained to the Brooklyn editor of the *New York Times* that the people in his area were not getting enough home relief (welfare).

My editor said, "See if you can find out from City Hall."

I called up and told the switchboard operator I wanted to speak to the mayor. She asked, "who was calling."

I told her, "Mr. Perlmutter of the *New York Times.*"

I was surprised to be immediately put through.

The mayor's response to me shocked everyone, including all the City Hall reporters.

"You have no idea how happy I am to talk to you. . . ."

And the mayor proceeded to unburden himself, for nobody had paid him any attention.

We ran the story on page 1 the next day.

Today you could never ask for the mayor and get to him. You would be connected to a press department.[39]

Mayor John O'Brien had also been famous for his malapropisms. He had displayed a mastery of the misplaced phrase, and the press did him a disservice by quoting him accurately. The result was that, by the time he also opposed LaGuardia in the 1933 mayoral campaign, his malapropisms were well-known throughout the city. The press concluded that, in spite of himself, Mayor O'Brien was fair game for entertaining copy.

The news cameras had also caricatured him. Failing to capture the mayor's alert blue eyes or affable expression, they distorted his large jaw, protruding brow, prominent bald head, and barrel-chested build. Cynical reporters at City Hall had their field day when he confessed: "Oh, I'd love to be a

newspaperman, because I love the classics and I love good
literature."[40]

When Fiorello LaGuardia won the election campaign of
1933, O'Brien wrote a message of congratulations to
LaGuardia then said to reporters: "The man who takes over
the City Hall now will have an easier job. . . . I ironed out the
worst problems."[41]

Mayor O'Brien had been incapable of perceiving the un-
intentioned humor of his utterances, and he especially could
have used a press secretary to control his statements, or
better yet, to reshape them.

FIVE

FIORELLO   H.   LAGUARDIA

Fiorello H. LaGuardia served as mayor of New York City from 1934 to 1945.[1] Because of his yen for publicity and knack for exploiting the dramatic and earthiness of life, LaGuardia is the most remembered of New York City mayors.

LaGuardia had always read newspapers carefully. He wrote in his autobiography:

It was during my boyhood in Arizona that I first learned about corrupt local government, and I got my political education from Pulitzer's *New York World.* We had two newspapers in Prescott, the *Journal Miner* and the *Prescott Courier.* These were typical Bret Harte Western newspapers, devoted mostly to local news. When the Sunday edition of the *New York World* arrived in Prescott on the following Friday or Saturday, I would rush to Ross' drugstore where it was on display. There I had looked at the first funny sections I had ever seen, featuring the Yellow Kid. From that comic strip came the expression "yellow journalism." I have enjoyed the comics ever since.

When I got home with the *Sunday World,* I would carefully read every word of the *World's* fight against the corrupt Tammany machine in New York. That was the period of the lurid disclosures made by the Lexow investigation of corruption in the Police Department that extended throughout the political structure of the city. The papers then were filled with stories of startling crookedness on the part of the police and the politicians in New York.[2]

LaGuardia was 18 when the 11th infantry had been ordered from Fort Whipple to Tampa, Florida for embarkation. Young Fiorello wrote the editor of the *St. Louis Post-Dispatch* and offered to be the paper's Tampa correspondent without salary if his fare from Arizona to Tampa were paid. The editor accepted, and LaGuardia began his newspaper reporting days on the Italian front in World War I.

The physical distribution of propaganda leaflets was one of his functions.

LaGuardia returned to the Italian front and completed his military experience–which had included public speaking, contraband-running in Spain, and intrigues against the political integrity of the Austro-Hungarian Empire–by flying the big Caproni bombers in the night-raids. . . . It was dangerous work, because by this time the Committee on Public Information had become impressed with the successful use of propaganda in Russia and believed that much could be accomplished by raining pamphlets over the Austrian lines. LaGuardia was given bundles of stale printed exhortations fixed so that the cord would break after they had fallen a certain distance and thus release a snow-storm of printed paper behind the trenches. The Austrians heartily disapproved of this idea and sent word that any aviators caught in this activity would not be treated as prisoners of war, but as spies.[3]

In 1924 radio was just coming into use and LaGuardia then turned to that medium to provide a forum from which he could broadcast his stand on prohibition, his advocacy of pacificism, and the other causes in which he had been most deeply interested. In December 1932 LaGuardia, under the auspices of the League for Industrial Democracy, called for a new economic and political deal.

In 1933 Fiorello H. LaGuardia ran as a fusion candidate against former Acting Mayor Joseph V. McKee, the latter running on the Recovery party ticket. Throughout the campaign, whenever the need had arisen, McKee had answered his critics that "newspapers now opposing [him] praised his record as Acting Mayor." McKee would quote an editorial that might indicate that he had tried to give the city an economical and efficient administration and had rebelled against Tammany bossism: "This testimony, ladies and gentlemen . . . was given only a few months ago and not during the heat of a campaign. I am the same McKee they spoke of then; I have not changed. . . ."[4]

But LaGuardia called attention to an article that former Acting Mayor McKee had written for the *Catholic World* in 1915 when he had been a high-school teacher. The article had questioned the moral and political reliability of New York City's Jewish youth.[5]

LaGuardia won the election, and on the day after the *New York Evening World* editorialized:

> . . . The *Evening Journal* believes that the new Mayor will devote all his energies, sincerely and earnestly, to the task that the voters have confided to him.
> And this newspaper will support the Mayor in all his constructive efforts.
> The most exciting Mayoralty campaign in New York is over. NOW FOR RESULTS.[6]

The *New York Evening Post* commented:

> . . . Mr. LaGuardia is not the answer to all prayers. Nobody ever had a right to think he was or is. Nobody ever is, anyway. . . . But there is one thing everybody knew from the start about F. H. LaGuardia. He is himself. There are no strings tied to him and leading back to somebody's nimble political fingers.
> He faces great difficulties. But we believe he will overcome them. . . . And that will be a great victory for himself and at the same time a great victory for sound, sane, constructive and economic municipal government.[7]

And the Greek-American newspaper wrote: "The *New Tribune* congratulates you on your overwhelming victory which bring honest government to our great city. . . ."[8]

When he went into City Hall that first day,

> The reporters streamed after him. To their shouted questions, Fiorello flung back only one sentence in Italian: "He says no more free lunch. Finished. The party is ended. No more graft."
> At 11:15 [first morning] . . . standing in a studio of NBC to speak directly to the seven million New Yorkers. The beginning of this new "nonpartisan" administration was a matter of such interest to the whole country that a special 45-minute radio program was transmitted

from coast-to-coast. "New York City was restored to the people at one minute after midnight."[9]

Walter Lippmann remarked in the *Herald-Tribune* only a short time later:

Mayor LaGuardia has taken hold in New York City in the manner of a man who knows what it's all about. His appointments are admirable. Not for twenty years has the city seen so able and experienced a collection of high officials or so many men in the responsible posts who are there by proved knowledge of the problems they had to deal with.[10]

LaGuardia's first term as mayor drew to a close; it became increasingly clear that there was no one in the city who could defeat him for reelection. Every important newspaper with the exception of Hearst and the conservative *New York Sun* supported him.

When he was reelected LaGuardia said "nobody wanted me . . . but the people."[11] The *New York Times* had given him a reserved endorsement saying "The continuance of good government in New York is the issue in the municipal campaign and Mayor LaGuardia presents this issue to the people."[12]

LaGuardia's press men, as Reporter Perlmutter called them, included James (Jim) Kiernan and Lester Stone. Kiernan and Stone were the publicity technicians; LaGuardia was his own senior press secretary. Lester Stone was listed in the New York City Green Book as one of the mayor's secretaries, but he also wrote press releases and maintained contact with the press.[13] Much of the general policy concerning relations with the press, however, emanated directly from the mayor. LaGuardia himself used newspapers to make headlines to manipulate the support of his concepts and ideas, even preparing his own stories to get his viewpoint across.

Ernest Cuneo, a reporter for the *New York Daily News,* observed first-hand LaGuardia's relations with the press.

Come to think of it, Fiorello was seldom charitable in his utterances concerning reporters or the press in general; and to the New York press in particular he was *never* charitable. He considered the Washington press to be of a higher caliber because unlike the New Yorkers, he said, they would respect an "off the record" statement. In fact, when holding a press conference in Manhattan, he would often say witheringly: "This is absolutely confidential and not for publication. So don't mention my name when you print it!" . . .

His sporadic forays against the fourth estate dated from its bitter assault on him when he first opposed the Sales Tax. A good many editorials had been absolutely scurrilous, even going so far as to question his patriotism. I'm sure this had hurt him more deeply than he ever let on; at any rate I know he had me clip and give him every abusive comment I could find.[14]

In another incident, Mr. Terranova had "sewed up" the artichoke market during LaGuardia's administration. The mayor went to the Bronx Terminal Market himself with fanfare and bugles at six o'clock in the morning to read a proclamation against the artichoke racketeers.

The hostile *New York Sun* made fun of this circus byplay, but missed the fact that while the mayor was telling the pushcart peddlers he would protect them by use of trumpets, his own law secretary was in Washington before the Department of Agriculture . . . to secure cancellation of Terranova's license to sell artichokes.[15]

Mayor LaGuardia turned out to be the greatest showman and the least inhibited chief executive ever to occupy City Hall. No other American politician of his time with the exception of Franklin D. Roosevelt made so much news. LaGuardia had steadily risen as a publicity value. On one occasion Congressman LaGuardia was to invite the newspapermen and photographers in to watch him make illegally intoxicating beer in his office. He then repeated the process at the corner of 115th Street and Lenox Avenue in New York City, told the patrolman he was making beer, and asked to be arrested. The officer refused to oblige, and the stunt was good for the front page in the news-scanty July days.

More and more, he had learned how to force through to the public his activities and point of view. In 1922, LaGuardia had been written about only 25 times in the *New York Times*. In 1924, he received 54 press notices in the *Times,* and so on until in 1937, he was receiving about 1,000 press notices a year. Many were front page news that served his efforts to

dramatize the administrative problems of a city of seven
million people.

In the course of this drive for public attention, he had
learned to use effectively all the devices by which a man
may break into the newspapers on his own terms. He wrote
vigorous letters to responsible public officials on matters of
current news interest. He made announcements and statements to the papers that had news value for their radical
sauciness, for their political independence, or for their
challenges to stuffed shirts. He introduced bills or resolutions
for inquiries in Congress that gave him a spring-board from
which to speak or write about the subject. He exposed such
wrongdoing as stock-market tipster activities or prohibition
enforcement methods. He staged stunts, such as his public
brewing of alcoholic beer already mentioned and his brandish-
ing of beef-steaks in the House of Representatives, to illustrate
his attack upon high costs of living. Despite occasional errors
of taste and judgment, he had made himself "news" and commanded free advertising for his views, which were the natural
expression of a fair-minded independence unusual in public
life.

LaGuardia had a number of newspaper friends: Paul
Anderson, *St. Louis Post Dispatch;* Ray Tucker, *Scripps
Howard;* Duff Gilfond, of the *Nation,* a periodical; and Frank
Tichener, publisher of the *New York Outlook.* Other newspaper friends also included through the years, Doris Fleeson,
Lowell Limpus, and Maurice Postley, and Ray Howard,
publisher of the *World-Telegram,* who had supported
LaGuardia for mayor in 1933 when all the other newspapers
in town had ignored the "little Reformer." His law clerk
early in the depression was Ernest Cuneo, a former cub
reporter on the *New York Daily News,* who in later years
wrote LaGuardia's biography.

LaGuardia used many of his friends as his informal assistants or advisors. They were drawn into decisions in many
capacities, some of which affected his press comments.
Judge Seabury often dropped into City Hall at the end of the

day and with LaGuardia drove for an hour around the
boroughs. Before going home, LaGuardia would stop off for
a cocktail at the Seabury town house. In the summer, they
met on Monday mornings at a gasoline station in the center of
Long Island, near Commack. Seabury would be driving in
from East Hampton and LaGuardia down from Northport.
Then LaGuardia would step into Seabury's limousine, where
they talked over municipal matters on the rest of the drive
into the city.

However, the Mayor's temper was short. George Britt,
staff writer of the *New York World Telegram,* had once
observed that "Getting a rise out of him is like taking candy
from a baby." One paper summed it up with "Our able and
tempestuous mayor was at his worst in his address to Board
of Alderman yesterday, and his worst can be very bad,
indeed."[16]

There was always a standing list of persons, city editors,
and columnists who could phone the mayor to get his views
on public issues.

When reporters would persistently question LaGuardia, he
would laugh off the question or snarl with anger, depending
on his mood. They enjoyed the game, however, putting the
aggressive mayor on the defensive. Many of the members of
the working press were less than charitable towards him. He
often managed to treat them rather highhandedly. They felt
that for a man who knew the value of publicity and had
remarkable skill in manipulating the power of the press, he
was not sufficiently fond of reporters. What disturbed them
most was his quick, fierce resentment of almost any kind of
criticism.

Irving Spiegel, who, at the time of this writing (May 1972),
is a leading *New York Times* reporter, tells the story when the
mayor asked him, "Well, Irving, what did you think of my
speech?" He replied that it had been a fine speech. "Lots of
substance, but there was one place where I thought your voice
rose too high." As Spiegel recalls it "The mayor fumed and
responded . . . "I was going to give you a lift downtown in my

car, but now you're on your own."[17]

LaGuardia's opposition to organized politicians was the issue over which the conflict between the Mayor and the City Hall press corps arose originally. During the campaign he, more than any one of the other candidates, had been most critical of his predecessor, Mayor O'Brien, for requiring the press to submit written questions. However, after being pushed by a reporter's question, LaGuardia also demanded that all questions be submitted in writing. This came about after LaGuardia had called the reporters into his office to inform them that "It will be a wholesome thing for all city employees to know and understand fully that for the next four years it will not be necessary to belong to a political club. It is no longer necessary to see politicians. All city employees need do for promotion is to do their work and they will gain promotion on merit."[18]

One of the reporters then asked "Was the Mayor forbidding all political activity by city employees?" LaGuardia had answered, "No, except that I would urge all city employees to quit political clubs." Finally, in an effort to secure a better lead for his story, one of the reporters asked point blank whether the Mayor "was indeed prohibiting all political activity by city employees." LaGuardia angrily retorted, "Are you trying to pin me down to a word? Are you trying to put words into my mouth?" And it was at this point that the Mayor henceforth demanded that all questions be submitted in writing.[19]

LaGuardia began to make Sunday broadcasts on December 21, 1941 on the city-owned radio station WNYC and continued without interruption until the end of his term on December 30, 1945. The opening and closing signature of the broadcasts was "The Marines' Hymn." Seated at his desk with a folder of documents and newspaper clippings, he would salute his listeners with the words: "Patience and Fortitude." LaGuardia's radio program became popular listening on Sunday afternoons, and he became one of the nation's most appealing political figures. The impact of his broadcasts became the wonder of the networks.

During the newspaper delivery strike of 1945, New Yorkers were entirely dependent on radio broadcasts for their news. LaGuardia, knowing that newspapers were also a source of entertainment, read the comic strips to New York's children from the published but generally unobtainable newspapers. Newspapers in the rest of the nation reported his performance with sympathetic amusement. The movie newsreel companies asked him to repeat it for them.

LaGuardia, through these broadcasts, led crusades against gambling interests, exploiters of the plain people, as he liked to think about it. A few of the newspapers began to level headlines at the Mayor, claiming his broadcasts included "Gestapo Tactics," "Un-American Tactics," "Children Asked to Complain About Parents," "Children: Inform Against Your Fathers." The mayor promptly responded with his personal touch: "Any editor of any paper who says that the mayor asks children to squeal on their fathers is telling a lie. He knows he is lying and he is printing and selling that lie for three cents a copy. That is pretty low."

Thomas J. Curran, New York County Republican leader assailed the mayor for his use of the radio station. "I think the people of New York City are just about fed up with the dictatorial arrogance of the mayor, who uses the Municipal Broadcasting System as though it were his own personal property. The spectacle of the Chief Executive of the world's first city making use of a facility of communication which is publicly owned, simply as a vehicle through which he can spew his venom over any person who dares to disagree with him is a disgrace."[20]

Regardless of the feelings that Curran and others held, WNYC became the direct link between the Mayor and the people of the City of New York. LaGuardia had recognized this fully.

I want to talk today for a few minutes about WNYC. I consider WNYC the most useful broadcasting system in this country, particularly at this time. I am sure that the various divisions of the Federal Government—the U. S. Employment Service, the Manpower Commission, the Army, the Navy, the OPA and the Public Health Service—will all agree to the very useful purpose that WNYC serves. New York City needs WNYC. I do not think there is any question about that. There is one thing I want to clear. I am getting sick and tired of hearing some people, very, very few, talk about the Mayor's use of WNYC. I have been in office for some forty years and even before we had radio, I was able to keep in touch with my constituents. I shall continue to do so. That is one reason why political bosses do not like me. I keep the people I serve informed and I shall continue to do so. I want to hear from you about these broadcasts, whether you like them or not, whether you want them. I have had many, many offers to go on a commercial station and if there is anything more said about the mayor on WNYC, maybe I will. I think I will send an offer to the Board of Estimate, and see what they say.

We got about 14 or 15 letters in opposition . . . so I have picked one of the milder ones. It comes from the Nativity Rectory, 20 Madison Street, Brooklyn:

"Your Honor:

Please give the radio and us a rest. You have convinced me, at least, that you are vain, conceited, and abusive. Why waste time proving what you have proven a thousand times? You might give us a farewell speech when your era of persecution is over. But make it short - please. . . ."

I will not be able to answer all of your encouraging letters but I want you to know that I appreciate them so much.[21]

Upon LaGuardia's recommendation WNYC also began to be used for political broadcasts.

. . . The candidates for Mayor will speak over WNYC. Last year I established the custom of giving equal time to all candidates without cost, on the municipal radio station. Not that it is the candidate who has the most dough, the most jack, who gets the most radio time. The reason I say dough and jack is because I want certain low-downs who are contributing that kind of money to know that I am referring to them. Big bums![22]

The mayor had also proposed to link the country's non-commercial radio stations into a new broadcasting chain, with New York City's municipal station WNYC as one of the links; this plan did not materialize.

LaGuardia had always felt that the press was an auxiliary arm necessary for administering the city and that publicity was an essential administrative mechanism for carrying out his

work. LaGuardia himself had recognized this in his regular
use of the radio, and sought to develop cooperation through
the press whenever this was possible. He did not feel that an
adverse relationship should exist between the press and the
executive arm of government. In reviewing a biography of
former Mayor Gaynor, LaGuardia had pointed out how he
had wanted to work with the press.

Review of "Gaylor" by Louis Pink

. . . reviews some of his policies . . . can convictions be secured, and the
criminal element, gambling and prostitution be suppressed without the
use of unlawful force or the employment by the police with the
wildest creatures of the underworld? . . . It can be done without
resorting to such tactics. That is what I am trying to do. That is why
I appeal to the press for help. . . .[23]

Mayor LaGuardia resorted to the press to publicize and
gain support for his noise abatement program. Lester Stone
was put in charge of the publicity campaign, but in the Sunday
broadcast of July 22, 1935, the Mayor also asked the public
to write in complaints.

A newspaper release was issued on August 11, 1935:

Preliminary to the introduction of a city ordinance on noise abatement,
an education campaign against unnecessary noises in New York will
be started next month by the City Administration, Mayor F. H.
LaGuardia announced.

Publicity included an extensive drive on radio, both the city
station and the local commercial stations, newsreels, and
newspaper articles. A general publicity committee was set up
along with separate local publicity committees. On September
29, 1935, the release from City Hall stated that the "Mayor
. . . will proclaim Noiseless Nights . . . in a direct radio appeal
to the citizens of New York City from his desk in City Hall."

Mayor LaGuardia may have thought that the press should
serve as an administrative aid, but he also thought the press
should be guaranteed complete freedom.

On the occasion of Newspaper Week, beginning on October
4, 1942, the Mayor stated the following:

This week is Newspaper Week in our country. It is of great importance because freedom of the press is one of the issues in this war. The American press has a great tradition. They were real pioneers who first started newspapers in our country—men who fought for great principles and men who knew how to fight. Let us hope that in the maintenance of the press in our country we will always have the same kind of sturdy, clean honest men who first published newspapers in the United States.

I do not know whether there is such a thing as an Oscar for fearless journalism and for the protection or for the courage to protect the rights of a free press. If there is such an Oscar, it would go this week to the *New York Times* for having the courage to resist the unlawful demand made by a combination of department stores. . . .

The *New York Times* lost some of its advertisements, but it retained its dignity and its honor.[24]

LaGuardia began his radio talk of Sunday, November 11, with the theme of "Peace and Democracy," explaining fully his concept of freedom of the press, use of newspaper headlines, and straw polls.

The backbone of democracy is a free press and now, of course, a free radio. It is just as important as freedom of speech, of course, and what amounts to freedom of speech, the right of assembly, the right of petition. But a free press indicates, of course, a truthful press. If the press is not truthful, it does not serve its purpose. It degenerates. In fact it serves an opposite, a destructive purpose.

I recalled that the infamous Sedition Act of 1798 was the last previous attempt to shackle the minds of the American people in the way we were trying to do it in 1917. I also pointed out that under the provisions of this espionage bill assistance to oppressed peoples in other parts of the world would be prevented, and if such an act had been on our statute books at the time, the Republic of Portugal would not have seen the light and the hopes of the Russian people would not have been realized.[25]

Mayor LaGuardia expressed many opinions concerning the press aside from stating its importance to his administration or the fact it should be assured its freedom. Following are some of his expressions on various topics.

If you do not like an editorial in the *Daily News*, the unfair editorials of the *Daily News* or the *World Telegram*, why not go out and get even with them and buy a bond. Don't you see, instead of buying the paper buy the bond.[26]

                                    . . .
I read in the papers that the mayor-elect has an office at the Commodore
Hotel. I think that is rather uncomfortable and I have written him that
we would be very happy to accommodate him here at City Hall.[27]
                                    . . .
   Here is another instance of lying in the press. I refer to the October
30, 1945 issue of the *Journal-American.* It is a sort of editorial entitled
"Misusing the Police." That was deliberate, that was an inspired
story. . . . But that article is very replete with misinformation and it
borders just enough to be untruthful and yet passable. For instance, it
charges the Mayor with assigning police officers. Well, that is a lie and
that lie was written to sell for five cents. Whom did you please by
writing that article, *Journal-American*? Are you trying to be like an old
paper that is not published now: you know which I mean, the *Evening
World,* and its relation with Arnold Rothstein? Is that what the
Journal-American is trying to do? . . . You made it appear as if eight
police officers were shot within the month. Well, that is another lie.
You took the figures of four years, and made it appear as if it happened
overnight. So that is what I mean by a press that is not a truthful
press.[28]

In one Sunday broadcast LaGuardia had referred to an
editorial in the *Long Island Star Journal.*

The Municipal Authorities will not issue working papers for teenagers
who want to earn spending money by setting up pins in Queens
bowling alleys.
   The *Long Island Star Journal* is a fine paper. I know the owner and
I know the publisher. They are very fine citizens. . . if he wouldn't
want his sons and I [LaGuardia] wouldn't want . . . what right have
they to ask the sons of other fathers to be a menial, picking up bowling
pins, so that someone can have a good time?[29]
                                    . . .
   I want to call the attention of students of journalism to the Sunday
Times and the Sunday *Herald Tribune.* In these two papers you will
see a very skillful approach to the issues, a very skillful use of headlines
and treatment of news articles. Very fine sportsmanship is displayed
in both papers and all within the rules of the best in journalism. I
want to congratulate both papers for the presentation and summation
of the situation as it appears to them at this date.[30]

On June 10, 1945 LaGuardia had congratulated the
Journal-American "and the splendid reportorial work of Leon
Racht," for investigating and reporting to the mayor about

certain violations in the city. It resulted in conviction and
jail for the offending party. One favor the mayor asked:
"Incidentally, Mr. Racht, I am glad that your picture was not
in the papers, or was it, because they are getting to know our
inspectors. Therefore if you find any other such place give
us a chance to make the arrest and then print your story."[31]

He had teased on the same broadcast that it is surprising
for him to express thanks to a newspaper.

Well I want to express thanks to one of our New York City newspapers.
That is rather unusual for me, isn't it. Well, where credit is due, it
certainly should be given, and I want to say "thank you and well done
to the New York *Journal-American*" for their work in finding a sort of
speakeasy of food.

LaGuardia had not hesitated to praise the newspapers, but
when he recognized distortions he responded publicly and
angrily, "Can anything in journalism be lower than that."[32]

On other Sunday broadcasts the mayor had read editorials
of the newspapers which had been published during the week,
and strongly took issue with their statements. More than
likely, it was the *Daily News.*

He also reacted when he learned that newsmen were guilty
themselves of wrongdoing. On one occasion he learned that
financial reporters for the *New York Times, New York
Herald-Tribune, Wall Street Journal, Evening Post, Evening
Mail,* and *Financial America* had received a total of nearly
$300,000 in gratuities from the publicity agent for pool
operators on the Stock Exchange, then under indictment for
fraud. LaGuardia then received a mysterious brown trunk at
the Washington, D. C. railroad station with an escort of
policemen. He deposited the trunk in police headquarters
with the comment to the clamorous newspapermen only that
he had some important papers he did not want stolen. What
was in the brown trunk? The suspense mounted that
LaGuardia might explode a bombshell at the Senate Committee
on Banking and Finance, which was investigating the miscreant
stock exchange.

The next day LaGuardia made his appearance between policemen carrying the brown trunk. While flash bulbs popped, the chest was placed under the committee table. LaGuardia then opened it and took out some papers. Holding up affidavits and newspaper clippings and canceled checks, LaGuardia charged the stock-jobbers of Wall Street with bribing financial writers of several New York newspapers to push certain new worthless securities.

LaGuardia had obtained his material from one of the bribers who had been indicted for forgery and was waiting trial. By scooping the capital and the press, LaGuardia turned the Senate hearings into a sensation. The stunt, like the beer-brewing demonstration of the previous decade, captured the imagination of the public for its sheer audacity. You've got to hand it to "the little Italian Congressman" wrote Will Rogers.[33] The mysterious arrival of the trunk, the cops, the police vault, the waving of the papers, the playing to the press and the public—all contributed to vivify in one dramatic incident the conspiratorial problems of Wall Street of that era.

LaGuardia had also defined "abuse" by the press after a situation had arisen in which a woman had complained that she had not been able to get a telephone after making an application to the New York Telephone Company.

Well, the Telephone Company is not to blame. My criticism was not directed against the Telephone Company. Now the paper will say tomorrow, "he didn't say but he hinted, he did not quite say that he was criticizing the court." Yes, I am criticizing the court. That is exactly what I meant to do. Now write an editorial about that.[34]

The foreign language press also was important to LaGuardia. When he was first promoting himself with the leaders of the immigrant community, LaGuardia had been behaving like his Irish counterparts in Tammany Hall, who had risen to political power in and through their own ethnic group. He had his speeches released to *Il Giornale Italiano, L'Araldo Italian, Il Telegrafo, Il Progresso,* and *Il Bollettino della Sera.* Nevertheless, the Italian language press had come out against

LaGuardia during the election of 1933 because many Italian-Americans had resented him for being a Protestant and a Mason. More specifically, *Il Progresso's* owner had idealized Mussolini and supported Tammany in return for rich contracts. However, the *World-Telegram* published an article on October 12, 1933, indicating that some Italians did support LaGuardia.

A resolution calling upon Italian language newspapers to reflect the political opinions of the majority of citizens of Italian extraction and to present more prominently and completely news of Fiorello H. LaGuardia's fusion campaign was passed last night at a meeting attended by representatives of about 600 Italian societies, it was learned today.[35]

LaGuardia also released stories to *La Prensa,* the Spanish language newspaper.

Mayor LaGuardia also had made statements to the press opposing the immigration laws, and he thereby gained the support of John L. Bernstein, president of HIAS (Hebrew Sheltering and Immigration Aid Society), and the Yiddish language newspaper *Der Tag.*

In a speech he made before World War II, LaGuardia referred to Hitler as "the brown-shirted fanatic who is now menacing the peace of the world and nominated the German Reichsfuehrer for a "chamber of horrors" in a building dedicated to religious freedom at the New York World's Fair. The German press called LaGuardia a *"lumpen."* LaGuardia retaliated with an untranslatable Teutonic insult against Hitler. Secretary of State Cordell Hull apologized to the indignant German Ambassador, but for the first time since the World War, Americans in Germany were treated with public contempt and hatred. The controversy raged for a fortnight and then was dropped by mutual consent in both countries. LaGuardia had scored an important political effect but at serious cost in civic dignity and public responsibility. Yet he had expressed the sentiments of great numbers of American liberals.

Aside from making broadcasts on WNYC and trying to gain the cooperation of the newspapers, LaGuardia also issued a municipal report in 1936 that listed the accomplishments of his first two years as mayor. It was given the rather formidable title of *New York Advancing: A Scientific Approach to Municipal Government—An Accounting to the Citizens by the Departments, and Boroughs of the City of New York, 1934-1935.* It also was launched with the usual publicity. On the December 30, 1945 radio broadcast LaGuardia announced that *New York Advancing* had been issued and that copies were available to all. "Yes, to political clubs, too. Write in and get a copy. I am sure you will all find it interesting."[36] Copy No. One was autographed by Mayor LaGuardia, "To the New York Public Library from F. LaGuardia, September 1936 . . . for all the citizens . . . present New York experiment is noteworthy—because it seeks to remove politics completely from the government of the largest city in the country."

New York Advancing opened with the statement: "To the victor belongs the responsibility for good government." Then LaGuardia listed the results of the first half of his four-year term: extension of civil service, divorcing the police from politics, appointment of what he felt were good men to the bench, savings in the Law Department, balancing the budget under the comptroller, completion of the city's subway system, reduction of interest, economies in administration, city bonds selling at 121, increased tax values, centralized purchases with consequent savings, improvement of piers, airport plans, plans for subway unification, cleaning out the racketeers in ice, fish, vegetables, completion of the Bronx Terminal Market, promotion of the World's Fair, special aid for children, slum-clearance and low-cost housing built with Federal funds, improved hospitals and prisons, enlarged cultural activities, scientific police work, better sewage disposal and street-cleaning methods, new fire-fighting equipment, planning for charter revision, for low-cost housing, for a municipally operated power plant, and for the establishment of a municipal art center, including an opera house, a symphonic concert hall and city auditorium.

Mayor LaGuardia also published "Lessons on Good

Municipal Government" in November 1937, which included
copies of newspaper releases written during the campaign for
the mayoralty of the City of New York between October and
December 1937. The mayor originated these "lessons" himself, based upon data prepared by an editorial and research
staff headed by Lester B. Stone. The lessons included a
review of the functions and accomplishments of the various
city departments.

LaGuardia had several purposes in mind in making public
these daily lessons. "For one thing certain of those on the
opposing ticket have an almost perpetual habit of misquoting
the facts." In addition, "the very essence of Tammany mal-
administration and corruption is the story of the Fusion's
administration's cleansing of the Department of Correction,"
he asserted, in making public the eighth of his series of
"Lessons on Good Municipal Government" for the "general
public benefit and the particular educational advantage of
the Tammany candidate."[37]

Although LaGuardia had attracted some national attention,
he was essentially of major interest only to the press of New
York City. However, a new city charter was put into effect
on January 1, 1938 that caught the imagination of the
country. Political writers from papers throughout the country
traveled to New York and interviewed LaGuardia. LaGuardia's
words about the charter when he took the oath of office for
the second time on New Year's day of 1938 were carried by
all the national press services. "It is not a charter for politicians. This charter will establish a very efficient machinery
of government. It will also be in existence long after every
man in office today is gone."[38] LaGuardia began to be
quoted more and more on national problems. At one press
conference, he termed himself, "A spokesman of the
American public."

LaGuardia's main tenet had been that an officeholder,
regardless of his level of position, must perform as a non-
political, nonpartisan administrator. This was the basis of
his faith in his ability to give good government. He had felt

that the reason William Jay Gaynor and John Purroy Mitchel, two of his predecessors as Mayors of New York, were not fully successful was that they gave politicians something or recognized obligations to politicians. He was fiercely determined not to make the same mistakes.

The *New York Times* declared as well. "he had combined the good government aspiration of Mitchel to many of the human attributes of Gaynor; his appeal is neither to mass or class, but to all those who, realizing the obstacles, want to see this city governed at once more wisely and more humanely."[39] The mayor was opening swimming pools, using the Police War Memorial Fund to build eight "memorial" playgrounds, bringing thousands of previously exempt city jobs into Civil Service, reclassifying, improving and reorganizing the Civil Service, and striving in the teeth of Wall Street to save money on electricity by building a municipal power plant. He cut his own salary from $40,000 to $22,500 a year to save money on the budget. He announced plans to reorganize the city's college system to provide special institutions for teaching technology and the science of government and had promoted a noise-abatement campaign to make life more tolerable in the crowded areas of the city's debilitated neighborhoods.

LaGuardia had never forgotten the importance of responding to the people. He knew that headlines in the *New York Times* are fine, but that, among constituents who rarely if ever read that very proper newspaper, the on-the-scene approach was more effective. There had been vigor in LaGuardia's publicity. LaGuardia had possessed qualities of boldness and determination that had infused his public statements. Above all he was a man of character, a genuine fighter, who had aroused the public and quickly dramatized issues of immediate concern to them and demonstrated that it was possible to make an effective assault upon political machines, if you knew you were right. To do this LaGuardia had spoken throughout the city in order to build up public support and keep his name alive in the newspapers. LaGuardia,

however, had an almost psychopathic inability to take criticism
of any kind. Although the New York City newspapers generally gave LaGuardia good coverage, the Mayor, in his turn, was
suspicious of and antagonistic towards them because they
might take him to task now and then. He deluded himself
into thinking the newspapers of the city were against him,
that they had things "fixed" to prevent accurate news of his
doings, that they emphasized the city's weak points instead
of its strong points. Because of this attitude LaGuardia
proved to be difficult to City Hall reporters. For a reporter
to ask the mayor a pointed question was often to risk an out-
burst of temper and tongue lashing; he had often used his
radio program to assail these newspapers.

Newsmen had enjoyed interviewing this explosive man.
He was what they called "good copy." He might have been
a trifle pompous on occasion but he was never dull. LaGuardia
was colorful, straightforward, quotable, and he made his job
more meaningful, dynamic, and vibrant for the media men.
It was always "a good fight" in the interests of free press for
both sides.

SIX

WILLIAM O'DWYER

William O'Dwyer served as Mayor of the City of New York from 1946 until the "Saturday before Labor Day 1950 when the mayor's resignation was filed with the Office of the City Clerk."[1] William J. Donoghue, a former news reporter, who was listed in the New York City Green Book as Executive Secretary to the Mayor, served also as the mayor's press secretary. As executive secretary to the mayor Donoghue who was flanked by a staff of five, arranged most of the mayor's appointments, sat in on all policy meetings attended by the mayor, arranged press conferences as the need arose, and wrote many of the mayor's press releases. He also supervised speech writing, answered the mayor's correspondence, and prepared letters for the mayor's signature. Donoghue also coordinated the press work of department press secretaries and/or the commissioners. If a problem arose which involved public information, a department press secretary would first discuss it with the mayor's press chief; regular meetings were not held.

Gabe Pressman, the veteran City Hall radio and television commentator, stated that, in his estimation, Donoghue should be considered the "first press secretary, and one of the best. The whole press secretary concept started with Bill

Donoghue."[2] Donoghue had a strong and commanding
personality. He enjoyed the confidence, respect, and affection
of all the reporters at City Hall. He had a great sense of the
press. Although he did not understand television, he prided
himself in adapting to this new media.

Donoghue served as the buffer and the liaison between the
mayor and the Room 9 journalists.[3] The reporters were
basically happy, because none was treated to an exclusive
story. Every reporter was given sufficient information to
write his story. Also, if there was a dull day for the reporters
and the mayor had nothing to say, Donoghue was resourceful
enough to have something of interest all the time.

Donoghue would arrange for the reporters to meet with the
mayor in the mayor's office and would have a story prepared
for them. Reporters, at Donoghue's urging, were often social
guests of the mayor at Gracie Mansion as well. Mayor
O'Dwyer himself arranged the appointments and invited them
to Gracie Mansion. O'Dwyer's personal secretary extended
the telephone invitations.

During the first year of O'Dwyer's administration New York
City celebrated its Golden Anniversary, which afforded the
mayor an opportunity to be widely quoted on the front
pages of the city's press. Numerous press releases were
announced by the mayor himself concerning the plans and
programs of the city celebration.

Mayor O'Dwyer has invited President Truman. . . .[4] All employees
of the city who have served 50 years, and all who have retired after
50 years of service will be honored by the city."[5] A record turnout
of members of the United States Senate and House of Representatives
is assured for the President's Day, Saturday, July 31. . . .[6] Jubilee to
include Ballet Style Show.[7]

Seventy-five newsmen were honored by the city during
the celebration.

Mayor O'Dwyer put his napkin by. The look of the Irish dreamer
swam softly in his eyes, and he told some seventy-five old New York
newspaper men, in tender Bohola blarney, that on the golden anniversary
of consolidation the city owed them a great debt.

"Where, gentlemen, in all this world, " he asked emotionally, "could you find a town of 8,000,000 like New York, that would let a man throw his shovel on the coal pile, to become the Mayor of the City?"

The glowing reference to his climb from laborer to chief magistrate of the consolidated city set the proper mood. Reporters who had worked here fifty years or more, pushed back the steins and conjured up mellow memories. [8]

Mayor O'Dwyer did not hesitate, however, to assail a newspaper when he felt it was justified.

The Mayor, at the rally and other campaign appearances, continued his attack on the *New York Sun,* assailed the *World-Telegram,* and declared that certain newspapers were "rags for the NAM" [National Association of Manufacturers] .[9]

Though the mayor believed that newspapers were generally not on the side of the people, on occasion it was his pleasure to quote the praises of the *New York Times.*

The Mayor quoted at some length from two *New York Times* editorials praising the record of his administration. After reading from one that cited his accomplishments in the fields of transit, education, hospitals, housing, health, garbage incineration, sewage disposal, in the treatment of civil service employees, and in the reorganization of city departments, the mayor demanded:

"Who said this? None other than the sedate and cautious editor of the *New York Times* in a lead editorial on May 27."[10]

The reporters in Room 9 had lauded Mayor O'Dwyer for years. During good times their stories had favored the mayor's image. The late dean of City Hall reporters, Frank MacMaster, had

. . . liked Mr. O'Dwyer best. He was an interesting conversationalist, had a good sense of humor, and could laugh at himself.[11]

There were conflicts in Mayor O'Dwyer's administration. The Kefauver Committee, which was the Senate Committee assigned to investigate political corruption, had repeatedly stated that Frank Costello, a reputed gambler, had been the power behind the city's Democratic party machine, Tammany Hall. In addition, it had been reported that Frank Costello had had conversations with Mayor O'Dwyer in the mayor's

home. At the same time the Fire Department had been
involved in a scandal. The mayor's closest friend, First
Deputy Fire Department Commissioner James Moran, was
tried, convicted, and sent to prison. It was under such circumstances that Mayor O'Dwyer announced his resignation on
August 15, 1950. (Simultaneously with his announced resignation, it was stated that Mr. O'Dwyer was to be appointed
United States Ambassador to Mexico.)

Vincent Impellitteri as President of the City Council
became Acting Mayor.

Everything is set today for the big farewell party the city is throwing
for its resigning mayor, William O'Dwyer. . . . As of tomorrow, New
York will have a new mayor—Vincent Impellitteri—who'll preside until
the November elections.[12]

During O'Dwyer's administration, the press knew more
about what was going on in the city than during any prior
city administration. Many times reporters would come into
the mayor's office and just sit around and talk with the mayor.
If a major issue were to be discussed, the mayor would hold
formal press conferences in his office as the issues arose.
Radio and television did not substantially alter the functions
of the press secretary.

As press secretary to the mayor, William Donoghue was
thought to be especially capable and astute. "He was considered one of the best men in his field," stated former
Mayor Vincent Impellitteri.[13]   After Mayor O'Dwyer's
resignation, Donoghue continued to serve as press secretary
to Impellitteri while he served as acting mayor.

SEVEN

VINCENT   R.   IMPELLITTERI

Vincent Impellitteri, president of the City Council when
Mayor O'Dwyer resigned, was appointed the acting mayor
and promptly announced his candidacy for the Office of
the Mayor.

Receiving the press in his old office filled with flowers, the new chief
executive of the city said that "God willing, for the next few months—
and I hope for much longer—I will devote every energy I possess to
the serious obligation of this important office.[1]

The Tammany Democratic party machinery had not
wanted Impellitteri for mayor. Nevertheless,

I only had less than five days to do it but I was able to get over 65,000
signatures in the required span of time and ran for mayor in the
election of November 1950 on the Experience party line.[2]

Impellitteri was the first person in the history of the city to
be elected as an independent mayor.

William J. Donoghue continued to serve as Executive
Secretary to Mayor Impellitteri after O'Dwyer had left.

Knowing of his background, experience and integrity, I knew if I took
him in as Executive Secretary he would give me the same degree of
loyalty he had given O'Dwyer. During my term as President of the
City Council I had come in contact with Bill Donoghue frequently.[2]

Donoghue also served the then Acting Mayor Vincent
Impellitteri in his campaign for the 1950 mayoral race.

As to Donoghue's service to the new mayor, Impellitteri
commented:

I do not know if anybody was better. He was of tremendous value to
me in all my mayoral administration and when I was president of the
City Council. . . .[2]

The secretary worked closely with the mayor, as Mayor
Impellitteri recalled.

Whenever Donoghue wanted to see me he would come in to my office
at any time, even in the middle of a conference. The door was always
open to Bill. Sometimes we had written memoranda; I don't remember
on what, but most of the time we did not. . . .
Bill Donoghue and I ironed out our differences. He always did what
I told him to do. Our differences might be political; it might be
something which happened in city government. He would discuss it
pro and con; sometimes I might change his thinking; sometimes he
might change mine.[2]

Donoghue also continued to act as liaison between the
mayor and the press corps, from whom he commanded the
confidence and respect of all the City Hall reporters. If the
mayor were free and reporters wanted to see him, Mr.
Donoghue would arrange these "extemporaneous" conferences as quickly as possible for the reporters.

Reporters didn't have to catch me on the steps of City Hall. They
always had free access to my office. If one newspaper cornered me and
he might want an exclusive, I would tell him that I would be in my
office and I would hold a press conference if anyone of them wanted it
together; then they would go to Bill to arrange it. I would never allow
one reporter to corner me on the steps of City Hall in the hopes of
getting an exclusive. I would say so that all of the reporters could
hear, gentlemen, I will be in my office if you want a press conference.[2]

The mayor had a definite conception of what should be
required of his press secretary:

The position of press officer is very necessary. It is indispensable. The
press secretary is a strictly personal appointee of the mayor. It should
be personal. He serves at the invitation of the mayor. He is there to

protect the mayor's image. He is there to protect the mayor. He is
working for the mayor; he is trying to protect a favorable image for the
mayor for the public. . . .

There was no organization chart which listed the press secretary. He
was known as Executive Secretary, as an aide to the mayor. Today
the veil has been drawn aside, and the executive secretary is known as
press secretary to the mayor. I don't think the press secretary position
is any different before me or today. . . .

I see the role of the press secretary as an indispensable part of the
mayoral administration. The mayor just doesn't have the time; he's
got to do research; the press secretary has to do research to answer
correspondence and prepare speeches. If anything today, the job for
the press secretary has multiplied since I left it. The only recommendation I could give a press secretary today is to work in the style of Bill
Donoghue and follow his example. However, today, to be a successful
candidate you have to use television extensively. . . .

I think the press secretary has to have a good working relationship
with the press. It is very valuable if he has had newspaper experience;
it is very valuable to have had experience meeting the public and dealing
with public relations. He must enjoy the respected confidence of the
press. He should be familiar with political imput rather than grow into
it. Essentially the press secretary starts off as a journalist and
necessarily becomes familiar with the political process. The job is a
combination of both political and journalistic input.[2]

Mayor Impellitteri saw his press secretary's responsibilities
as a "tremendous job," and "a daily asset to the operation."[2]

The mayor also had Donoghue attend all of the policy
meetings, in part, perhaps, because he felt Donoghue had
an uncanny ability to find out what was going on in the city.
The mayor felt that

I was the policy maker, but he was the technician. If I wanted advice
I would outline my thoughts to Bill and he would give me his
opinion. . . . He would discuss the situation that arose. Bill would get
a lot of feedback which he would share with me.[2]

Donoghue also sat in on many of the meetings of the mayor's
administration. When a commissioner was confronted with
a problem, he first would discuss it with Donoghue, who
then might arrange a meeting between the commissioner and
the mayor. Donoghue knew about all appointments and
arranged many of them. (The mayor often received appoint-

ments at Gracie Mansion or City Hall early in the morning when he did not want the public to know about them.)

Press conferences were arranged by Donoghue almost every day at City Hall. Any time the news journalists at City Hall wanted a special press conference, they would go into the press secretary's office and say they wanted to see the mayor. Mr. Donoghue would set up the conference in the mayor's office, usually for the same day as requested. Reporters had complete access to the mayor.

My door was always open to the reporters. They had to go to Bill Donoghue to clear the time, and it was theirs when I was available. We usually did not know in advance what questions the reporters would raise.

There was generally a big difference when TV came in. You pretty much knew in advance what the broadcast journalist wanted to talk about. With the news media they seldom let you know in advance what they wanted to talk about. Mr. Donoghue could not "fish it" out of them.

The reporters would try to pin the mayor down on an issue on the spur of the moment. The reporters at City Hall in those days were pretty sharp. You couldn't get a question from left field.[2]

The reporters never forced the mayor to take a stand; however, they did force premature disclosures.

Something might be pending in a department and I didn't want to release it till I checked it. One of these fellows might get a tip and I would be put in the position that I had to reveal the information I had not wanted to state. I didn't use "no comment" because that doesn't satisfy an astute reporter.[2]

When asked how he was prepared for a press conference, Mr. Impellitteri stated that the press secretary would talk to him about some of the questions that might arise especially "if Mr. Donoghue had an inkling of what the reporters wanted to talk to me about."

I tried to cultivate and encourage the support of the press on a particular issue. I would issue press releases stating my position and the position of my administration on a particular subject. . . .

No press release would go out without my ok. I saw every press release. It reflected the thinking of the mayor so I didn't permit it to go out without my authorization.[3]

The mayor preferred press releases rather than writing letters to the editor, as some earlier mayors had done, because he felt that "was an idle gesture. The papers didn't have to publish a letter. . . ."[2]

Mayor Impellitteri used the press to gain the opinion of the public concerning a possible decision or policy:

I might be thinking of giving a top job to gentleman "A"; I might feel he is the proper person; I would discuss this with Donoghue; this is what I am thinking of doing, what do you think the public's reaction will be?

I have never used the press to hold back news, but I might use the press to float a trial balloon. For example, when I was thinking about appointing a police commissioner, a man I selected was Tom Murphy who had a brilliant background in the United States Attorney's Office. I decided he was the man for the job. I put out a trial balloon; it was very well received.

I did the same thing with the Fire Department, which had been rid of its scandals. I decided to appoint a person not politically close to me and a member of the Republican Party. He was also Jewish. I selected Jacob Grumat. I picked him so that no one could say I was trying to cover up any of the scandals that were in the Fire Department. Mr. Grumat had also been from Tom Dewey's office. The feedback was excellent on this balloon.[2]

Mayor Impellitteri also held background briefings with publishers and editors, usually at the publisher's office. Most of those papers had an editorial board, and "on frequent occasions I would meet with them to give them my thinking on certain views."[4]

As acting mayor and during his campaign for election, Impellitteri decided that radio was the best means of reaching the people directly.

Acting Mayor Impellitteri introduced his new police commissioner, Thomas F. Murphy, to a television audience tonight on the WPIX program, "At the Mayor's Desk." Impellitteri took the occasion to express faith in the integrity of New York's police as a whole.[5]

The mayor frequently spoke over commercial radio stations in the city, as well as the city-owned station, WNYC.

The mayor's first in a series of TV broadcasts began June 9, 1953 on television station WPIX.

At one time WPIX made available to me a weekly program where I could air my views, outline my plans and present my department heads. I used television to go to the public and let them know what was going on during my administration. It was a live program. On the city-owned station WNYC, I had a weekly taped show which could be replayed.[2]

The mayor's speech writer would seek the opinion of the press secretary, but he worked directly with the mayor. He would prepare a draft, the mayor would go over it, and the speech writer would prepare the final copy.

The speech writer worked closely with press secretary Donoghue who sometimes prepared an occasional speech.

In general, however, whenever I had to speak in the evening, I usually only had my chauffeur and a police aide. I might have three or four speeches to make that evening. Not unless I had a specific reason did Bill Donoghue come with me in the evening. The ground work had been laid before I left City Hall. Many of these speeches, in fact the vast majority of them, I delivered extemporaneously. The press releases, if necessary, had been drafted before I left City Hall.

Many of my speeches were well documented. If I spoke before the City Chamber of Commerce, for example, and I talked on city finances, there was a lot of research and it was well documented. On the campaign trail Bill Donoghue and my driver went with me.[2]

The mayor also spoke at many meetings of Italians, Jews, and Greeks, among others, and then issued press releases to the ethnic newspapers. The mayor also publicized his trips to Italy and Israel to bolster his coverage in the ethnic newspapers.

I was invited to Italy and went also to Israel, because many of my constituents were Jewish. There was a press man with me on this trip. This was in 1951. Pictures had to be taken. There was scheduling of conferences and ceremonial programs. I really needed my press secretary because they kept me going from 8 in the morning till 11-12 o'clock at night. Sometimes I spoke extemporaneously; sometimes I had to make a formal address. My press secretary was of big help.[2]

Generally speaking, Mayor Impellitteri said the press had treated him fairly. His relations with some individual reporters had been excellent, although most New York newspapers had not supported his candidacy for mayor.

I tried to treat all newspapers alike, but I must say I had a feeling of appreciation for what the *Daily News* did for me. However, that could not affect my fair distribution of what all the newspapers should have.

You must remember that some of the news media are politically oriented, politically motivated, and favor certain political parties. Sometimes their news coverage is affected by their editorial policy. The *Daily News* is favorable. They supported my candidacy. It was the only paper that did. No other newspaper thought I could possibly win. I was drawing big crowds when I spoke. The last few weeks of the campaign, the *Daily News* ran a poll and showed me ahead.[2]

Mayor Impellitteri also thought highly of Paul Crowell of the *New York Times,* who had an intimate grasp of the city government.

He was 100% on the level. He would write a story whether or not it met the editorial policy of the newspaper. He and Donoghue were very friendly. Gabe Pressman was also another fine reporter.[2]

The mayor would socialize with reporters at outings, dinners, Christmas parties, and the program that the press and the chief executive hold, the annual Inner Circle Dinner, and a joint baseball game.

Impellitteri did have some difficulties with the press. For example,

One of the difficulties with the press in my administration was that I had considerable opposition on the Board of Estimate. The county leaders were not happy with my election. My job was much more difficult, particularly as a result that most of the newspapers at the time had indicated I had lost my independence. I had become a party mayor. I had aligned myself after my election with the Democrats in the hopes of cementing former ties and getting a better working relationship in Albany. So the papers were making problems out of the situation.[2]

Donoghue served the mayor in his relationships and dealings with the press, and he transmitted the mayor's message with minimum distortion. There was a strong mutual respect between the mayor and Donoghue, although they were not personally intimate. Donoghue also was respected by the journalists, because he understood their needs. Donoghue was a classic press secretary, who performed well the technical requirements and activities his assignment demanded.

EIGHT

ROBERT F. WAGNER

Robert F. Wagner was mayor of the City of New York from
1954 to 1965, and had four press secretaries during his four
terms of office. William R. Peer served from 1954 to 1959 as
secretary to Wagner and was in charge of press relations.

I had been over in Brooklyn working for Abe Stark, then the Borough
President. Some people had recommended me to work for the city
ticket. It was good therapy for me, for I had just lost my son in upstate
New York. After Wagner won, he and I went down for a vacation to
Lord Beaverbrook's in Nassau; I had been announcing the appointments
for commissioners for Wagner's administration from there. One day
Lord Beaverbrook asked the mayor, "Do you have any more appointments to make?", and Wagner immediately replied, "Bill Peer is going
to be my press secretary," and that's how the mayor asked and told me
at the same time. Beaverbrook, responded, "Good luck, fellow press
man." I said to Wagner, "Why did you say that?" . . . and Wagner
replied, "Bill, it's the best thing for you. I need you." And Bill Peer
replied to Wagner, "if you every make me ashamed of you, I'll leave
so fast you'll never know what it took." I was a rough, tough uneducat-
ed man. I never went to high school.[1]

He had had wide experience as a newspaperman and in
publicity. He spent ten years with the New York City News
Association and shorter periods with the *New York Post* and
the *New York Daily Mirror*, where his assignments included

coverage of municipal affairs and politics as well as general finance and business.

Peer was born in Brooklyn and had studied evenings at New York University. In the early nineteen forties, Mr. Peer served as confidential assistant to two Manhattan Borough Presidents, Stanley M. Isaacs and Edgar J. Nathan, Jr. He had also assisted Thomas E. Dewey in his successful campaign for Governor in 1942. Mr. Peer then worked in the successful campaign of William O'Dwyer for mayor in 1945. From 1946 to 1953 he ran his own public relations business. In 1953 Mr. Peer was at Mr. Wagner's side at the primary and general election campaigns. His cheerful, breezy manner and helpfulness made him popular with newsmen.

Bill Peer maintained that it was necessary for the mayor to have a press secretary. If he did not, too much of his time would be taken up with the press. In addition, he felt the mayor did not understand the requirements of the press and he did not understand the techniques of making information available.

Peer also felt that the press secretary had to be completely dedicated to the career of the mayor.

My responsibility is not to the public but to my principal. You learn to interpret to the public to the advantage of your principal. Although I am very concerned with people it is my principal's praises that I must sing.

My job was to make the Administration look good. Wagner had won the 1954 election with the major city newspapers against him. They had editorially endorsed his Republican opponent, Harold Riegelman, and "had wanted to see us flop."[1]

In the 1954 mayoral race Wagner had been called by his opponent "Bubblehead." After Wagner was elected, Bill Peer's first job was to convince the public the mayor had a good mind and get rid of that image.

Peer set up a regular television program called *The Mayor's Report,* insisting that the mayor appear alone without a scrap of paper before him. The mayor would then be questioned by a panel of reporters on the issues of the day. City Commissioners asked to appear along with the mayor. Peer would say, "No, another time." He tolerated no delusions of his image-making of the mayor.

Peer recognized his results had been successful when Bernard Baruch called to say "Yes, he [the mayor] has a good mind." Another telephone caller said, "This guy [the mayor] is not as stupid as I thought."

Peer was successful in dissolving the image of Wagner's being only the son of a famous father. The second successful step in the image building strategy was to "move on into the personality aspect to present him as a man" of broad competence in his own, not filial, right.

Peer, however, did see his role as a service function to the public, but not necessarily in the providing of information.

Your family is the people. Anything that is going to hurt the public as you see it and you will not be a party to it, then you must either change the policy or resign. Once policy is made, however, and you strongly disagree with it, then you have no other choice but to resign. If you're a snob, apart from the public, and keep yourself separate from them, your usefulness is destroyed.

. . .

The ideal press secretary has an insensitive hide which encapsulates the public official and protects him from the onslaughts of the press and public disapproval. He's an intellectual and spiritual bodyguard. He's the court's son-of-a-bi - - -; he's the whipping boy; he takes the beatings that rightfully belong to his principal. Buffer is a weak word. He's the official son-of-a-bi - - -; the blame taker, the punch-taker, the pain-taker. It's no job for a man who has concerns about himself.[1]

Peer also maintained that the press secretary should be a generalist and have strong political input. "He's got to have political input; he'd be lost without it. The press secretary must have a certain wittiness; a lack of snobbishness, social, financial and educational." A press secretary should be a newspaperman, Peer thought. "If he's not, he's going to find hostility."

Peer felt the press secretary had to attend council sessions, if not as a participant, at least as an observer. Otherwise, a press release could not be given its proper perspective. "My title of executive secretary was whatever you made of it."

The job could be one of considerable power and influence or one could be a "coatholder or mechanic" such as Peer considered Frank Doyle to be. "He would sort of hang around the mayor, hang his coat. He had some sort of patronage title."

As executive secretary to the mayor Peer felt that he was hierarchically above the deputy mayor and his relationship to the mayor was on a one-to-one basis. Peer maintained that there was no "proper order" to the functioning and ordering of press relations as he had established them; he considered his operations to be administratively loose.

One of his administrative functions involved the mayor's commissioners and illustrates how the secretary worked in relation to the mayor and the press:

I was friendly with most of the commissioners, although I was rough with some. I fired three commissioners without the mayor's permission. I told him after it was a fait accompli, I had to do this, for the mayor was a vacillator. I knew things had to be done.

If I cared about my own personal popularity I couldn't have done it.

One commissioner was telling the press he hadn't resigned. I said to the press, "Oh yes, he had." Wagner said, "You shouldn't have done it." Others said, "What else could you do, it had to be done. . . ."

I called together the press secretaries of the different departments, and I told them that "Anything good that happens in your department has to be reported in the mayor's name; anything bad would be their own problem."[1]

Rarely did the mayor and Peer communicate by telephone, nor was there any use of interoffice memoranda.

Peer would usually begin his day about 8:00 A. M. when the chauffeured city car drove him to City Hall.

I was always first. My days couldn't be planned, because I did not know what was going to happen that day. A demonstration could happen; a transit strike could erupt. If it were a transit strike, we would never go home. We would stay through and I'd sleep on the floor. The pressure of the office was greatest during the difficult times of strikes and other crucial atypical situations.[1]

If it were an average day, Peer would leave about 8:00 in the evening. During "normal" days Peer would arrange for press

conferences, if reporters came to him to see the mayor. Peer
first would explain to the mayor what he expected would be
discussed and give the mayor the facts he thought would be
needed to answer reporters' questions. Then Peer would open
the conference by making a statement and guiding the meeting
by questioning the mayor himself on the issues they were
willing to talk about. The discussion then would follow on
the desired subjects. Peer also directed the writing and publishing of press releases, most of which were handled by his
assistant, Jeffrey Roche. Releases were made on Monday,
following the belief of Theodore Roosevelt, who thought he
would have better coverage then because of the supposed
dullness of the weekend news. Peer also preferred to make his
statements in the mornings, because the reporters of the *New
York Times* attended for that rather than the afternoon
editions. (Peer also considered that Mondays were the best
days for him, whereas Fridays often were the most difficult,
being filled with unexpected happenings.)

Peer's attitude toward newspaper reporters was affectionate
and warm, although he was coolly professional to publishers.
inviting them to lunch to inform them of a variety of
situations, but introducing his statement brusquely with, "I
think you should know this." In turn, he considered the
reporters to be fair in their reporting of the news. Further,
he felt that he was regarded by the press corps as one of
their own.

We would go out to lunch together. I had been a newspaper reporter
on the city *Daily News*. Often a reporter would come to me. I've
got to get it, it's a must. They would ask you a question which I didn't
have the answer. I would have wanted to help him, but if I went beyond
the actual knowledge we would be in trouble.[1]

Mr. Peer was willing to grant exclusive stories to the
papers:

I would protect a man who had an exclusive. He would ask me for
verification on it. I would do it only for him and no one else.

The *New York Times* was more important than the *Daily News*. I would give certain stories to the *New York Times*. There were things I would rather have break in the *Times*.[1]

However, when he was asked if reporters ever had preferential access to the mayor's thinking, Peer responded:

The only one I can think of was Paul Crowell [of the *New York Times*], whom I trusted implicitly. He was close to so many mayors; he was intelligent and had much integrity. No one could attain Paul's knowledge of city government. I opened doors for him when he was working.[1]

To the other extreme, Peer sometimes withheld information entirely from the press, with the statement, "No comment." Sometimes he asked the press to hold back the news on difficult problems. At other times, he might release only some of the facts to test the public's opinion on some policy before it would be made official.

Peer was abused occasionally by reporters. For example, the *New York Daily News* attempted blackmail. The *News* wrote a series of stories about unauthorized welfare benefits, based on information supplied by Dominick Ramone, a Department of Welfare investigator.

Ed O'Neill of the *Daily News* came to me and in front of Ramone said, "My desk has told me to tell you if you don't lay off Ramone we'll smear you in your marital troubles."

I said to Eddie, "I don't hire and fire commissioners. There's only one answer to take back to your city editor. F - - - Y - -." The *Daily News* smeared me.[1]

On another occasion, the *New York Herald-Tribune* decided that Peer "was the bag man for Wagner."

They had assigned a very big reporter, Robert Bird, who reported back to his paper "I can't find any signs of it. I've known Bill for 20 years. I've never known him to be a crook."[1]

. . .

One day David Wise of the *Tribune* wrote a story about me. Knowing they had deliberately changed the story he told them to take his byline off.[1]

Peer's relationship with the mayor was based on mutual respect, although sometimes when he was told the mayor wanted to see him, he would jokingly say to the secretary, "Send him in!" Peer claimed that his feeling towards Mayor Wagner was a paternal one. "Although I was only five years older than he, when we were alone, I called him 'Kid.'" (Publicly, he called him "Mr. Mayor.")[1]

Sometimes Peer disagreed with what the mayor had to tell him. He would respond, "Kid, you don't know what you are talking about."

When I discussed policy the mayor had wanted adopted, I'd fight him all the way down to the ground if I disagreed. Commissioners used to ask how I felt about things to get the pulse of the situation.[1]

I asked Peer to recall his "biggest problem" in his relationship with the mayor. He immediately replied: "The weakness of my principal," which arose from the mayor's shortcomings, and Peer recalled one vexatious situation which had affected the mayor that Peer had to untangle. King Saud of Saudi Arabia had been invited to the city through a statement of welcome by the mayor. The news broke in the first edition of the *Journal American* under Harold Harris' byline. The difficulty arose because the invitation was deemed particularly offensive by many New York Jews in view of the unending Israeli-Arab confrontations in the Middle East. Wagner's constituency included a large Jewish population whose sentimental attachments toward Israel vaulted the entire episode into the realm of deep-seated emotional reaction: a politician's nightmare.

I was stunned and had not known anything about it, for the mayor had made the statement at a dinner affair the night before, in a chance impromptu remark.[1]

The next morning the reporters asked Bill Peer about it. He said he knew nothing about it.

I asked Wagner. "Did you say this?" It was true that the Mayor had a drinking problem; he would say these things, and then black out.[1]

The mayor answered, "Well, I guess I did say that. I'll bring the press in and tell them I said it and I meant it." Peer never allowed that. The mayor finally asked, "What do I do now?" Peer responded, "You go back to Gracie Mansion and have a virus for ten days." The mayor did just that. Peer went on television to counteract the story, suffering denouncement by those who admired the King.

This was an event by which Peer could have been destroyed professionally; the United States State Department might well have become involved and insisted that the mayor welcome the King. Peer admitted, "This was one of the dirtiest, toughest jobs I had to do."

Peer also was Carmine DeSapio's political confidante at City Hall. "He and Wagner had quiet sessions together but their meetings came through me." DeSapio was, it is generally agreed, a most powerful political figure, not as an elected official, but as a clubhouse chieftain in the tradition of Tammany Hall.

Another important person in the city whom Peer had to reckon with was Cardinal Spellman, Roman Catholic Archbishop of New York and ranking prelate of millions of American followers.

When Cardinal Spellman was on the phone, you bowed down. He was the power house. To carry on in government administratively you have got to carry on politically. You can't separate them.

Wagner would start the trouble and then I would have to develop the press support. Once Wagner said, "Bill, don't believe everything you read in the papers." I responded, "But you do . . ." Then Wagner kissed me, and said, "On you I depend."

Peer recalled that he replied, "But don't sell me down the river."[1] The personal life of your principal could make life hazardous for the press secretary. Sex and having bad friends was an occupational hazard of politicians. Wagner had his share, and many of these friends wanted something from the mayor. Some of them may have wanted nothing more than to reiterate the next day, "When I was talking to the mayor last night, I told him. . . ."[1]

This aspect of the mayor's life was made hazardous for Peer, to some extent, because the mayor's bodyguards see

everything, and it was the press secretary's job to maintain
friendly relationships between the guards and the mayor's
office; there is always danger of blackmail.

Peer saw the role of the press officer in the office of the
mayor as a changing process, altered by the mayor and the
man, rooted in their attitudes toward each other. "Indeed,"
said Peer, "I couldn't be John Lindsay's press secretary; and
Tom Morgan, I wouldn't let him shine my shoes."[1]

Peer stressed that there have been changes in the role and
functions of the press office over the years.

It is very definitely different in respect to the people with whom you are
doing business today. Now your reporters are a lot of kids out of
college.

The press secretary's office, though, will always be a public
relations department to enhance the image of the press secretary's
principal. This is a tough job. If you can't go with it, you quit.

Frank Doyle had been a newspaper reporter when he was
asked to become press secretary to Mayor Wagner, succeeding
Bill Peer. Doyle had served sixteen years with the *Daily Mirror*
before going into city government. He resigned from the
Mirror to become Press Secretary of the New York City
Police Department from 1946 to 1954, where he established
the world's first Bureau of Police Relations. Police officers
were prohibited from talking directly to the press, and all
communications came through the Bureau of Police Relations.

I had established pretty good rapport with the press at that time. It
helped me when Wagner was looking for a press secretary.

Prior to joining the mayor I had also gone over to the Department of
Sanitation and headed their community relations set-up. I had been with
city government twelve to fourteen years before going over to Wagner . . .

After Wagner's 1961 campaign I became executive assistant to the
mayor. I was put in charge of that office.

Professionally, I had met Bob's qualifications. The same thing can
be said for his other appointees, Debs Myers, Leslie Slote; also Bill
Peer. Among us four, I considered myself the closest personal friend
of Bob Wagner. That didn't mean we coupled together; we didn't have
that kind of relationship—Susan, Bob, my wife and I. We had a long,
warm friendship, although I was not his drinking partner.[2]

Mayor Wagner realized that the press office was a vital and
highly sensitive operation and an important arm of his administration. Frank Doyle would walk into the mayor's office
whenever he felt the need. Sometimes his secretary would
say when the mayor was calling, "The boss is on the telephone."

Publicly, Doyle always called Mr. Wagner "Mr. Mayor."
Otherwise he called him "Bob" or referred to him as
"Wagner."

Our relations with each other were professionally intimate but not
personally so. We did not socialize in each other's homes. Bob Wagner
was a Yale man; I was from St. John's of Brooklyn. On a personal basis
Bob Wagner's friends were Yale men, not even Harvard men.[2]

Doyle maintained that the position of press secretary was
necessary as far as the public was concerned.

A liaison office from the mayor to the press is necessary; otherwise who
would the reporter go to for information? The press secretary job is
quite important. It is important to have someone there to speak for the
head of government. . . . My general philosophy was to try to keep the
fellows in Room 9 knowledgeable as to what was going on in the
mayor's office.[2]

He thought that the press secretary should be both a
generalist and a specialist. Knowledge of journalism helps.

You could be a good public relations person, but unless you know and
realize the importance of deadlines and getting certain types of stories
to newspapers, all the great work you do might be lost. Understanding
the need for and recognizing deadlines are so important,
    I really think some of a working reporter's background is needed;
you understand the needs of the journalist, such as the pressure of
meeting daily deadlines.
    An important qualification of a press man is to know all the angles
of a press operation. We're trained right from the start to pick up
"the future box"—we've got to think ahead for the mayor, but the job
depends entirely on the man who hires you. You're the mayor's
appointee, and shouldn't be legislated in, for the mayor would have a
hell of a time getting rid of the person he couldn't work with.[2]

As executive secretary to the mayor, Doyle functioned as
the mayor's press secretary. He began a typical day at 9:00

A. M. at Gracie Mansion by attending meetings with the mayor, department heads and representatives of civic organizations. Then he would drive to City Hall with the mayor in the latter's car at about 10:00 A.M. Regular City Hall press assignments began on arrival and lasted until about 7:00 P. M.

At home Doyle would get calls about 6:00 or 7:00 A. M. from the afternoon newspapers: "Frank, this thing broke, what does the mayor say about it?" His comment usually was, "As soon as I can get comments from the mayor I'd be glad to answer", or sometimes he would give the reporter an answer and be quoted as "spokesman for the mayor." As press secretary, Frank Doyle did not do much writing. He sometimes prepared a press release, but usually they were written by Jeffrey Roche, however, who was the assistant press secretary and carried the title Director of Communication. He worked most of his time with the radio and television journalists. Speechwriting was separate from the press secretary's office, although the speech writers and the press secretary worked in close cooperation with each other.

I was the channel to the press, to the media for anything produced by Warren Moscow or Julius Edelstein, speech writers to the mayor. I knew what they were writing about. They would consult me on certain phases of the mayor's talks. Sometimes we would all sit together.

Mostly, however, Doyle's responsibility to the speech writing operation was consultative.

Doyle believed his official and administrative title of "executive secretary to the mayor" encompassed greater responsibility than "press secretary." And as executive secretary he did act as executive assistant to the mayor, which gave him more power and authority to aid the mayor in transmitting memoranda, orders, and directives.

To be officially the "executive secretary" is a hell of a tough spot. You're asked questions, and you're on the spot, "Hey, Frank, you're the boss - you call the commissioner," and *you have to call the commissioner.*[3]

The executive secretary had to be like a watchdog exercising the function of "oversite." This is one of the reasons I would be in a position to call in the public relations people from the other city departments.

There might be rumors from one of the city departments or maybe from the public generally that conditions in the building departments aren't good and that the inspectors are shaking down the landlord. I would have to try to get as much information to him in order to have an effect on the situation. When I was down there my office worked closely with the Commissioner of Investigation . . . we worked on a number of investigations together, and the press were pleased.

When information came to us through the Director of Markets that the people were being cheated by gasoline stations, we turned the information over to Commissioner of Investigations Louis Kaplan [Frank Doyle called him Lou]. Lou would report back to me. I would be guiding him as to whether or not we would call the press. We would then be in a position to develop good publicity for the Administration.[2]

Doyle also saw himself as one of the advocates of policy- and decision-making because, as a member of the mayor's cabinet, he sat in on all meetings. He said, "I didn't make policy, but I did participate in policy-making meetings."

In spite of his other duties, Doyle acknowledged that:

Your prime purpose directly is to get out the good news your boss wanted circulated. When you have a bad story someone accuses your boss, the Mayor. You've got to get the explanation and check whether there is any fact to it. You've either got to deny the situation or explain it, but it has got to be handled one way or another. Your only public position is to explain why certain things happen. There is no question about it, but this is both a public relations and publicity job combined. On the public relations end of it, as a former press secretary here in the city, you can't fool the press, and you can't give them a line of baloney. They are too able and too capable.[2]

Doyle maintained that even though a story may be un-favorable, tell it fairly and honestly, even though you may have a bad story tomorrow. That's better tactics than generat-ing series of bad stories and having reporters digging for information you deliberately were not giving them.

Doyle also organized and held briefing sessions regularly. If the mayor were issuing a statement to the public, Doyle would call the press into the office in advance of the release date, along with those involved in the story, to talk generally about the situation.

The press preferred these briefing sessions. They certainly didn't want to sit in on any session where they couldn't quote the official directly. These briefing sessions were more or less informal.

We held these briefing sessions whenever they were required. Quite often we did hold them with Wagner present. It depended on the number and the frequency of the releases we were getting out and the issues involved.

If Bob Wagner met with the housing officials and wanted a new public housing project, I might call a briefing session. I would give the reporters a copy of the release and answer questions.[2]

Press conferences were held twice a week, usually on Tuesday around 11:00 A.M., and on Thursday around 2:00 P.M. Thus the morning newspapers and the afternoon newspapers were satisfied. On several occasions the mayor held two press conferences in a day.

Doyle maintained that Mayor Wagner was one of the most accessible of public officials. Reporters would stop him as he came up the broad steps of the Hall. "I finally implored the press to let them let the mayor get into his office." (Wagner always wished to accommodate the press.)

Newspaper boys spoke to the mayor in the mayor's office. Then the mayor would go to the Blue Room where the electronic media was set up. He didn't want to hold up the newspaper reporters. Around 25-35 reporters and photographers covered the mayor.

Sometimes we would ask the newspapers to cooperate and hold back on certain disclosures in the press. For example, there could be a police investigation. The Police Commissioner would inform us that the disclosure of certain facts would hurt the investigation. On behalf of the Mayor I would call the newspapers and ask their cooperation to hold up a story.[2]

Wagner had a great number of newspapermen with whom he was friendly, including *New York Times* reporters Clayton Knowles and Paul Crowell. When Paul Crowell wanted to have lunch with Wagner, the mayor would oblige and not ask Frank Doyle about it.

The press secretary would arrange for reporters to meet individually with the mayor, who was available to the press every day. First the secretary would learn what particular issue the reporter wanted to discuss, and then arrange the appointment. Before the meeting Doyle would then brief the mayor concerning the kinds of questions he might expect.

Sometimes the mayor held background briefings with publishers and editors of the newspaper, radio, television, and magazine people to present his side of the story. In certain cases the mayor would invite them to Gracie Mansion.

Usually Doyle would consult with the mayor while he was preparing a press release. It also was necessary for Frank Doyle or Warren Moscow to call department commissioners who might be involved to get information. Then the press release would be written. The mayor might see it before it was released; more likely, he did not. Then Doyle often would call the reporters into his office to make a statement about the issue, rather than issuing a written version.

Doyle might issue exclusives, but he would not give a story exclusively to a newspaper man, if in his opinion the story was a "spot news" story, such as one that the mayor was going to announce that day.

I would never give that exclusively to a newspaper. I would be hurting the mayor's relationship with the press, particularly if I'm working with the reporters in the field. It would have to be a feature story for a feature writer, not a spot news story.

He also would leak some proposal or policy that the mayor was considering to reporters. At one time, for example, the mayor had been considering Newbold Morris as Parks Commissioner, but he had not been quite sure about the appointment. Doyle enlisted a friendly reporter and leaked the information that the mayor would probably appoint Morris; the reporter on his own then wrote the story. The Wagner Administration watched reaction from the people and press. If the feedback had been bad, the mayor would not have appointed Morris.

Sometimes the press secretary's office planned letters
to the editor, particularly to the *New York Times,* on crucial
issues affecting the city or a policy of the mayor. The press
secretary used a list of names over which he sent these
letters; they were usually those of people who were relatives
or friends of staff people.

Until the Wagner Administration, television representatives
were not recognized as "working press" in New York.
Television news programs were commercially sponsored, and
previous administrations had classified broadcast journalism
as a commercial enterprise. Mayor Wagner recognized
broadcast journalists as working reporters. (Gabe Pressman
was the first television reporter to cover City Hall and Mayor
Wagner.)

This change of policy did present Doyle with a problem,
however.

The press secretary has got to be in a position of being judge of the
activities and operations in the news gathering field. When television
reporters first came on, there were some problems with the pencil
press, particularly in conducting press conferences. The newspaper
reporter did not want to participate in news conferences with the
television crew.

Doyle thought that the press secretary should serve as the
direct link between any elected official and the press and
ultimately the people. The press secretary definitely should
provide information to the public in his highly sensitive job
which required constant attention to all statements. To
some extent Doyle believed the press secretary should over-
see the activities of those working in the city government
for the public benefit. Doyle strongly felt that his job
involved public relations. The Mayor of the City of New
York was more newsworthy than the governor or the
president he felt; thus the mayor's public relations needs
were greater locally.

The public relations staffs of the various city agencies
would check with Doyle, if they had any story which affected
the mayor, as the press secretary to the mayor coordinated

about thirty agencies. When a departmental release was issued which affected the mayor, such as snow removal, the press secretary wanted the mayor to come out "smelling like a rose." This was sometimes difficult. The public relations image of the mayor depended on the image of the departments at work. Also, if the mayor received correspondence pertaining to a certain department, he might turn the letter over to Frank Doyle. If it dealt with the Sanitation Department and the collection of garbage, Doyle would then send it on to the Commissioner for comments and recommendations. Were a subject pressing, he would call the Deputy Director of a department, using his title of executive secretary to bypass the department's public relations chief.

I found out when I came into the Office that you have press men and public relations men in practically all of the city departments and agencies. . . . These people in the departments usually had the administrative title of deputy commissioner or secretary to the department. Many of the fellows who handled the press secretary functions were former newsmen or radio and television people. They ran their own particular shops as part of the overall pattern of the administration.

I used to meet at least once every few months with public relations or publicity people in departments and agencies, which were responsible to the mayor. I had an open-door policy as far as the daily operation was concerned. If the Health Department had a problem and I felt the mayor should be filled in, I would call the Commissioner to discuss it. It was a question of coordination and ironing out certain situations.

I would make the determination that certainly the mayor's office wants to know about it.[2]

Doyle also accompanied the mayor on his trips.

You would have to be there to help him so that you could call the press people to meet him. When the mayor attended national conventions my main purpose was as a political liaison. This was because of my political contacts as a former newspaper reporter.[2]

Mayor Wagner, according to Frank Doyle, was interested in particular types of conventions such as those of municipal officers, finance organizations, the United State Conference of Mayors, and policy organizations. If the mayor were delivering a major address at any one of these conventions, his secretary became even more necessary.

Usually Mayor Wagner decided where he would speak. There was little or no consultation with his press secretary staff on what organizational dinner and meeting invitations to accept. However, if the mayor declined an invitation, the press secretary wrote the letters turning down the invitation.

The press secretary's office generally arranged the mayor's appearances. The speech writers in consultation with the press secretary wrote the speeches.

Doyle maintained a wide-open door to reporters and they often would call him to get the mayor's policy on a variety of matters. Doyle felt that providing Room 9 for reporters in City Hall was essential.

This location is a very close link for the mayor to the public. If the mayor can go 50 or 60 steps to the press office particularly during an emergency, this is a tremendous asset to the city.

During Bill O'Dwyer's tenure as Mayor there was a blackout. It proved essential that the press room be located in City Hall. All you had to do to get to the reporters was walk down the hall with a candle and give the reporter the messages.[2]

Doyle noted that when he had served there was "more press coverage of City Hall."

Today you have less newspapers and less coverage. Today you don't have the coverage of years ago. Today there is also much more image-building than in my time.[2]

He also noted that later administrations placed greater emphasis on community and weekly newspapers, supplying them with more material for feature stories than he or William Peer were ever concerned with.

Doyle recommended that:

... we combine various public relations officers throughout the city which would be responsible to the Administration, rather than shooting off through all different angles. It might be cheaper to have one central agency under control of the Administration.[2]

Doyle acknowledged that he had tried this to some extent, "but it unfortunately is a long drawn-out thing such as who should pay for the salary of the press secretary: the media or the mayor." Doyle acknowledged that, since the media act to some degree as watchdog for the public, he could not be of service to the mayor "if we were paid by the media. We are working for our boss."

Debs Myers had been a former newspaperman and public relations expert. A onetime *Newsweek* managing editor, Myers had a genius for helping politicians.

Mr. Myers according to those who worked at City Hall at the time, was not able to transform Mr. Wagner into the darling of the news media, but the phrase "bungling Bob" seemed to appear less frequently.[4]

He stated he had "the ability to turn lemons into lemonade."
Myers worked for Mr. Wagner from 1962 to 1964 before leaving (with a brief return in 1965) to enter private public relations. Whatever his title was—press secretary, executive secretary, assistant—Myers tried to keep himself out of newspapers and off television. "In government," Myers once said, "most of the so-called hidden persuaders would do better to remain hidden."[5]

I remember Debs. We had more purpose, of course, working with him. We'd always make the very first edition of the paper. Debs always called up the city editor if he had felt there was a "lousy headline." "Where'd you get that?" he'd ask, and you'd get it changed. You really got a feeling that the press didn't want to cross him at City Hall. There was a tendency to see editions of papers altered because of Debs' call.

When Debs was there he was called the executive secretary to the mayor. It was an interesting position. Frank Doyle was strictly a press secretary. He preceded Debs. Debs wanted to upgrade the title. There were interdepartmental conflicts and disputes. Commissioners were going off half cocked. Debs Myers wanted to beef up the role of the man trying to create the mayor's image. Originally Wagner had not had the confidence of Debs because he did not know him. . . .

Wagner was usually talking to the commissioners themselves and did not have enough time to get involved with the press problem. In 1962, Debs' first act was to call in all the press men in each of the

departments and kind of lay down the law, and above all to protect
the mayor. He pointed out to them that they had two bosses, their
own commissioners and the mayor. They could promote their own
boss but never at the expense of the mayor.[6]

When a reporter wanted to see the mayor, Debs Myers
would say, "I really want to get you all in, but you've got
to give the Mayor time. Give him a little breathing space,
fellows," and Debs would say, "which one of these ought I to
let in?", and Leslie Slote (another assistant at the time) would
then say "Well, this guy cut our balls off last week." Debs
Myers would go into Room 9 and say "I'm sorry I am a
bastard, fellows, but I can't do anything about it. The mayor
will only see one of you." Debs' own personality made the
job easier.

Debs Myers was not an intellectual. However,

Debs had very good judgment. Whatever the action taken it would
appear on the front page of the *New York Times*. "My only interest
was what it was going to look like on the front page of the *New York
Times*," he said. "I don't give a shit if its right or wrong." . . .

The judgment between the mayor and Debs Myers was constantly
being built up. Sometimes when someone was threatening the mayor,
Debs would say, "f - - - him." Debs knew the powers of the mayor's
office. He could jolly the mayor and reporters, too. Debs knew he could
tell a reporter he wasn't going to see the mayor. The guy was left to
meet with a minor functionary, that the mayor was too busy to see
him. Debs' comment would be, "f - - - him, but do it nicely."[6]

He could provide advice for the mayor as well. For
example, Gilhooley of the Transit Commission objected to
the plan to put police on the subway. He was doing this to
get publicity for a chance at the mayoral nomination.

Finally Debs Myers said to Wagner, "I really think you ought to get
those cops on the subways as fast as possible. Gilhooley ain't gonna
let up." It was a half minute of advice; the Gilhooley balloon was
totally cut. . . .

Debs Myers never worried about his role. His job, he felt, was to
solve a problem, not to make it. If you've got to worry about the
feelings of the press secretary then you can't handle the job. Debs
Myers was a problem solver. "Bob," he said, "my only job is to solve
problems. You really ought to see this guy."[6]

Debs Myers was never fearful of commissioners, who would come back to Wagner; in fact, Myers would often clash with a commissioner. A commissioner might say, "Who the hell are you, are you the press secretary?" and Myers would reply, "No I'm not, I'm the executive secretary."

Ordinarily a press release would not be cleared through the mayor. It would usually be cleared by Debs Myers or Leslie Slote, his press assistants.

Debs Myers really worked hard to transcend being simply a press secretary. He finally did become a political aide and a trusted friend of the mayor.

Every mayoral press secretary interviewed in this study voted Myers the best "back-up" man in the business.

According to Emanuel Perlmutter, *New York Times* reporter, the first press secretary who had power was Myers.

Before that, a guy would see that the press got releases and if the mayor had his speech ready. It wasn't a question of whether or not this was a major or minor role; the man would be an asset to the mayor if he had the ability to help the mayor work directly with the newspapers. If you are the hand taking care of xeroxing alone, you could be useless.[7]

Leslie Slote had been an assistant to Frank Doyle, then to Debs Myers, and then was appointed press secretary himself in 1965 having the title "press secretary to the mayor." Slote's background included being a reporter on the newspaper, *The Chief.*

Mayor Wagner in his third term brought in Debs Myers as his executive secretary. Myers, however, had no municipal experience, and so he went to the deputy mayor to ask who could help him get organized; Leslie Slote was available.

I got a call to go over to City Hall. The mayor had spoken to my boss, who was Maxwell Lehman and who was the deputy city administrator. They asked Mr. Lehman if I could be borrowed for a couple of days. After one day, Debs Myers said, "I want you to stay here permanently," so I went over to the mayor's office. I had been a senior management consultant for six years in the office of the City Administrator. I was always on loan. I took the office title, Assistant to the Executive

Secretary. Then Debs quit at one point, and I became Acting
Executive Secretary. In 1965 I became press secretary.[8]

Slote was assigned the ordinary routine public relations
work that involved securing newsworthy information from
the city agencies, preparing press releases, and supervising the
mayor's schedule.

He was given the special assignment of writing some of the
speeches for the Metropolitan Regional Council, an inter-
governmental body designed to improve the conditions and
services among the states (and some municipalities) of New
York, New Jersey, and parts of Connecticut. He also would
make an initial screening of ceremonial functions that involved
the mayor's presence.

He was given the responsibility of maintaining relations
with press secretaries of executive agencies, usually on an informal basis. "The only problem you might have would be
with the commissioner who was trying to build himself a
name." The commissioner wanted to do a particular thing and
Slote could not stop it, but "as to the mayor, we had verbal
contacts. I would walk into the mayor's office in the
morning."[8]

Leslie Slote had not been a political appointee and was not
even a reformed Democrat. Therefore, he was always suspect
by the regular party apparatus. Wagner himself never knew
how to evaluate Slote. That he never had the mayor's complete confidence, Slote maintains, was accordingly under-
standable. Slote was not part of the mayor's circle of close
friends. "We liked each other, but we were not intimate."

Slote did not consider himself an administrative officer
but an advisor to the executive. He felt he best served by
presenting the facts on events truthfully to the mayor.

Slote felt that hiding bad news from the executive was
not helpful. If there were a bad editorial in the *New York
Times,* he would go into the mayor's office and say "Look
Mr. Mayor, you got hit today." He never believed that, after
presenting the mayor with bad news, the mayor would think
Slote was not doing a good job, and, as an advisor, helping to

evaluate the facts to come to a decision. For example, should the mayor take a stand on Vietnam? There were political considerations; the hard hats were involved; would this hurt the mayor's chances of being reelected? In another instance, should the mayor take a position that might alienate the Catholics? He was involved with another problem when, working in the city administrator's office, he had dealt with reports about the ethnic composition of New York schools. Projected data showed half of the New York City schools would be nonwhite in ten years. This situation became exceedingly important when Slote was in the mayor's office, and it became necessary to develop communication with various new people and agencies. Slote pointed out from his analysis that the ADC program (the Aid to Dependent Children) also would be enlarged, and he also alerted the Administration to this related problem.

In one instance, Slote attempted to maintain silence when George Lincoln Rockwell, the late controversial American Nazi Party leader had wanted to speak at a public street corner, necessitating the need to obtain a city permit. Slote stated, "I was a member of the New York Civil Liberties Union. As advisor to the mayor I knew this would alienate and hurt him politically. I kept quiet and did not advise the mayor which direction to take. I presented both sides of the situation."[8]

The structure of the office included the press secretary, the assistant press secretary, and occasionally an appointment press secretary. In the later years of Wagner's administration, Mrs. Jane Kalmus was the coordinator of radio and television, the first person to hold this assignment. Slote believed that it was a mistake to segregate radio and television from the news print journalism.

Because he was an advisor to the mayor, as well as serving as press secretary, Slote believed that the single most important quality a press secretary should possess is commonsense. The press secretary should be a generalist, but he should, Slote thought, have some understanding of the problems and requirements of journalists and experience in the political environment. If the mayor was going to run for reelection, the press secretary should certainly have some comprehension of journalism, for election time was the busiest time for his office, and the volume of news releases was increased greatly. Of course, he also should have some real campaign experience. If the press secretary were to be a specialist as a journalist, however, he might lose sight of many more vital political problems.

Along with serving as an important advisor to the mayor, Slote felt the press secretary had the important responsibility of providing information to the public and getting a sense of public opinion (for which Slote used public opinion polls.)

As to speech writing, he felt that the speech writer should be a part of the press secretary's office. But this, too, revolved around the personalities of those concerned. In the past, the speech writers had been administratively separate from the office of the press secretary.

Slote thought that the press secretary also had to watch for inefficiency and especially corruption. When Debs Myers or Leslie Slote heard any breath of scandal, they dashed into the mayor's office to tell him he's "got to fire that man." Mayor Wagner's administration, particularly the last, "was pretty clean" according to Slote.

The press secretary became the second most important person in the office, Slote said, the first being the deputy mayor. And Slote reported to the mayor, not to the deputy mayor. He did note, however, that this arrangement depended upon cooperation between these three individuals. The press secretary, if he is good, is the first one to know "if there is a problem."[8]

Slote maintained that it was not important to be concerned whether or not the press was fair or if it were friendly or not. However, he did not believe that there was steady opposition press. One newspaper might be against Mayor Wagner one year and support him the next.

They have a job to do, and sometimes their missions conflict with our objectives. But our attitudes would depend upon the guys who were covering the mayor. I would say that the reporters and I were not that close. Some of the reporters, of course, like any other relationship, I had become friendly and personal with. Charles Bennett of the *New York Times* was one. He was a leading city reporter. He slept at my house the night my daughter was born. Basically the press secretary has got to get along with all of the reporters.[8]

However, the press secretary would thank a publisher or reporter for a favorable story from time to time, a matter of maintaining friendly relations.

Most of the reporters did not ask Leslie Slote for an exclusive press story because the answer always was no.

In addition, Mayor Wagner, through the press secretary's office, often would decline to have luncheon with a reporter. In some instances, however, the editors of the *New York Times* would be granted exclusive interviews with the mayor, but if it were done for the *Times,* the *Daily News* would demand similar privileges. Slote did treat one newspaper differently from the others, of course, for the *New York Times,* the *Post,* and the *Daily News* are three very distinct newspapers. Also he treated reporters differently. For example, Slote sometimes held back news from a reporter if he felt he had been abused by him or did not like him.

Sometimes the story on the city budget, for example, was given to the newspaper in advance of publication, so the reporters could study it. An embargo, however, was placed on its release. The editors of the *World Telegram* in one instance, decided not to honor the embargo.

We got around it by not giving it to the *World Telegram* till the last minute. What the press secretary thinks is important, the reporter may not, so we've got to place an embargo on the release on certain information.[8]

Slote noted that the technique of releasing a news story as a leak was used frequently to highlight it.

The best way to kill a guy is to leak that Joe Smith is about to be appointed commissioner. The mayor hated to have stories leak out before it became a fact.[8]

And in contrast, the newspaper reporters sometimes were asked to hold back news on certain occasions. On a very personal level, the reporters did this when Mrs. Susan Wagner was critically ill with cancer. The mayor did not want his wife to read the article in the newspapers or hear about it on the radio or television.

Also, there were times when Slote deliberately blocked the press to protect the mayor, although basically it was impossible to keep the mayor away from the press. The mayor cannot hide: You can always see him coming out of City Hall. Sometimes, however, a reporter might not hold back news of a political nature. It depended on the story and the relationship of the participants.

Slote seldom asked a publisher to support the mayor's view in a column:

You might call someone one day and call his attention to a particular issue, but I don't believe it is the press secretary's function to ask the press to support your principal.[8]

Slote maintained that never once did he use the technique of sending letters to the editor to get across a particular view on an issue. Sometimes he would ask a columnist to present some tentative policy to the public as a trial balloon to determine whether it would be accepted.

Slote's approach to a press release was to keep it short and simple. Major press releases were approved by the mayor and then distributed to the reporters in Room 9. Slote maintained there was no "best time" for issuing press releases; it depended on the circumstances. He never felt comfortable setting down rules and procedures for handling press conferences. He referred to the Washington background briefings held in the press room of the White House, maintaining that these kinds of briefings were very manipulative and that the press secretary was aiming at presenting predetermined issues. Slote did not want to be in a similar position.

The press secretary's conference would be held once a
week in the Green Room at City Hall.

I understand that in the old days under Mayor O'Dwyer's administration
the press conference was held in the mayor's office. It also took place
in the mayor's office in the beginning of the Wagner administration.
With the advent of radio and television, it was no longer possible to
have the press conference in the mayor's office. Of course you lost
the intimacy of this kind of conference. You couldn't schedule the
conference any longer on an impromptu basis. So we turned to a once a
week kind of operation when the press boys would want it.

There was no reason not to have a press conference, because the
reporters could get your man in the hall any time the mayor passed
through, but something had to be done in an orderly way.

I would go over with the mayor beforehand the questions that might
arise during the press conference session.

Wagner liked the reporters very much. He never felt uncomfortable
with them. Lots of times we had to work late at night, such as when we
had a newspaper strike. Wagner would come in and kid with members
of the press secretary's office.[8]

Slote was confronted with the problem of accommodating
both the newspaper reporters and those from the electronic
media at the press conferences. One day a *Daily News* top
man called Slote to complain about the presence of the
television men:

The cameras and the mikes are destroying the intimacy of the press
conference. The newspaper guys thought they were threatened. No
one has ever really worked this out. Every press secretary goes through
this aspect where the press believe the press secretary is either pro
newspaper or pro TV.

I tried to be fair, however; no one has worked out the perfect
formula requirements for TV and radio. It boils down to the newsmen having confidence in you. I believe I was able to get that degree
of confidence.[8]

The biggest problem Slote saw for himself on the job was
telling the reporters not to pressure the mayor on a particular
issue or at a particular time.

I would go into Room 9 and say to the reporters there, "The mayor is
exhausted, just leave him alone. I'm not going to be there; give the
guy a break."

However, when a story involving a serious scandal broke, for example, there was no "control," but the secretary could attempt to minimize what was happening.

In addition, Slote could not counteract major criticism of the mayor most of the time; he could, however, at certain times overcome adverse publicity by issuing news items that were favorable to the mayor.

You've got to protect the mayor. You must distinguish which is legitimate and which is useful. A good press secretary would have to judge before a *fait accompli*. It is a life and death responsibility to judge people, to be sensitive to them and their motivation. Understanding these people is an important aspect of the press secretary responsibility. You must not try to cover up a bad story once it has already been revealed. You fight the bullet. You must quickly handle any kind of scandal. The longer it drags out, the longer it is in the press, the more problems you have. You must try to end it in one day. If the press has confidence in you, they will treat the situation as an isolated incident.

Slote felt that he should have set up more background briefings between the mayor and publishers and editors, but it was difficult to do. He recalled the following story: The welfare department was threatening a strike. "I had arranged for Mayor Wagner to appeal through television to the welfare workers not to go on strike. The mayor was sensitive to the problem. I arranged for live television which was not easy to do."

Slote then went to Julius Edelstein, who was a speech writer and told him he needed a live television script. Slote stated:

I am prevented from doing anything, I'm not the speech writer, but Mr. Edelstein had not prepared it on time. I had wanted to be able to give the press an advance for the next day.

Wagner was in a box. I finally prepared the speech and gave it to the mayor.

The press secretary has to take the initiative and be a little machiavellian by exposing the mayor to the press when he feels that the mayor must take a stand on a political issue when he has been equivocating. I had a certain philosophy about this.[8]

"There is continual confusion in America as to what are the responsibility and the role of press secretary. Technology has taken over and the means became the end," Slote maintained.

If your man has long-range views, manipulation is inevitable, but the degree of manipulation is a consideration. Whether that becomes an end as I think it has with the Nixon people, determines the social responsibility of the administration.

The office of press secretary should not be legislated into the mayor's office; it is a personal thing. If you are a press secretary to Mayor Lindsay or Governor Rockefeller, you are practically living with your principal.[8]

Nevertheless, Leslie Slote had looked at the journalists as people who have to make a living, and he had to serve them. To that end he recommended flexibility in the operation, both in serving his executive and the press with sufficient sensitivity to avoid a credibility gap.

Paul Bragdon had been a lawyer before joining the mayor's office, and he had served as Wagner's Albany legislative representative. He was invited to be the press secretary when Leslie Slote resigned to become Governor Rockefeller's press secretary. At the time, there were five months left of Wagner's term. Inasmuch as the mayor had no long-range political plans, it was decided that Bragdon would terminate the press secretary's duties for Mayor Wagner.

Bragdon worked well with the press, for he knew many reporters from his trips to Albany. He believed that the press secretary operation was essential to the mayor's office. Mr. Bragdon also knew that, although press secretaries often share a common philosophy, they do differ in their approach to the job. A press secretary must know the mechanics of the news business, how to meet deadlines, and when to distribute releases. He must know how to get along with the press personally.

The case study of Woody Klein who was press secretary to Mayor Lindsay is an example of a press secretary not being trusted by the press. There was unfortunate publicity in the process. This was turned around by Harry O'Donnell who succeeded Mr. Klein. He had the personal rapport. Even though he was a reserved man, he kept counsel with every member of the press. Both he and Debs Myers had certain marks in the trade, which included their personal hobbies of collecting memorabilia and pictures of ships and baseball. Both men had a level of camaraderie with the press and the people with whom they were working. The element of joshing was a condition of their being able to do the job well.

The role depended in knowing how to manipulate. One can say in its crudest form that the job involved manipulating and fooling the people. If you don't sing along with the press, the press will murder you and your principal. You have to be enough on the inside to know what is going on.

Newspaperman love to drink with the fellows. This kind of camaraderie and warmth is what makes a press secretary have even a more direct relationship with reporters; he becomes one of them from time to time although the distance of his job is always maintained.[9]

Bragdon said, "I don't really have to be a newspaperman." In the old times, of course, newspapermen were offered this job much more often than they have been lately. Now the press secretary should have a concept of government. He should understand the staff role. One cannot really get into that job without being sure of the ground work, for whenever one spoke for the mayor, whatever was said became the mayor's answer. "No comment," when a comment was necessary, was not satisfactory either, for it bespoke hidden statements and feelings. However, at times all press secretaries did evade a response. In contrast, when some event that would become important was developing, Bragdon would tell the reporter, "I think you would care about this particular story." The *New York Times* was given preferential treatment by the press secretary: the *New York Times* reporter was *always* fully briefed because he was completely aware of how the *Times* would react. Bragdon regarded himself, in addition, as one of the policy administrators of the administration, in the sense that he was giving advice on substantive matters to the mayor and to other departments. The press secretary must coordinate the information that flows out of government to the press and from there to the public.

The press secretary cannot be neutral; he should fight like hell on
substantive issues, and if necessary should call up and give the commissioner a piece of his mind if he believed certain things were not correct.
But to the public, the press secretary must be partial. You do try to
conceal issues or problems that can create a habit in the office. If you
get wind of something, you ought to protect the administration, to
keep things from happening so it won't be on page one. The press
is a servant of the mayor. First the mayor; second, the press, and the
public third. The press secretary's job is to cast information from the
most favorable light.[9]

The stature of the press secretary depended on the personality and the dominance of the man he was working for and
how others viewed the press secretary's access to the mayor.
This depended on the character of the mayor. The personality
of the press secretary also affected his stature, as well as the
relationship between him and the mayor.

The trick was you had to seem to have others think that you were
speaking for the mayor. Your response might be that it is the mayor
who wants this. Not necessarily would you be saying it, but you have
to demonstrate the authority that others think you have by your
relationship with the mayor. This authority is not formal; it is assumed
authority that you have with the mayor; in reality you have developed
it on your own initiative. This is important when you have to call up
a commissioner and attempt to put out a brush fire.[9]

Bragdon's production staff turned out releases and also
wrote speeches for the mayor. (Knowing that the mayor was
resigning many of his special assistants had left for other jobs.)
There was an appointment secretary. There also were four to
six people working in Bragdon's office who, among other
things, wrote proclamations and messages that would be
released without consultation with the mayor. As a result,
there was a certain amount of rivalry between the press
secretary's office and that of the deputy mayor.

The administrative aspects of the press secretary's job
included the mechanics of scheduling the mayor's appointments and speeches, of coordinating the press relations from
the various departments and other agencies of government,
and processing and analyzing the mayor's mail. The press

secretary's office also prepared the mayor's year-end annual interview with the press. Press conferences also were usually held on request if the mayor had time. The television press conferences were frequently held in the Blue Room at City Hall. If a press conference was scheduled for the day, Bragdon would suggest reviewing the background briefing. Sometimes questions would be suggested to the reporters by the press secretaries, and reporters might ask in advance that certain information be covered. This was helpful, particularly if it were important to the mayor that he respond on certain topics.

Periodically Mayor Wagner would also have lunch with editors and publishers of the major newspapers of the city.

Most news that is reported on the government, Bragdon noted, is not a record of what government is doing.

What you get is measured performance. It is the rhetoric of top officials, mainly talking about political issues. And secondly, most reporters are interested in conflict. Even the *New York Times* is concerned with political combat. Very rarely do you get a measurement of government capacity.[9]

In return, the mayor often was blamed for everything. The TV questions are sharper when addressed to the mayor. However, Bragdon believed that the writers of television editorials were superficial. He characterized them as simply making a quick response similar to a newspaper "letter to the editor." They are really pugnacious, Bragdon asserted. The conflict was due in part to the fact that "the press is juvenile."

If you watch a press conference, you will note the same questions can be asked eight times. The reporters are sort of trying to dig in to get in all of the proper words. The endings are good, but you might end up with a very sharp, but not necessarily accurate statement. The press is looking at your operation as an adversary. This of course, does not necessarily enlighten the position of those involved but it does create conflict which is necessary for the reporter to write the more exciting story.[9]

Nearly every political problem was assigned to the press
secretary. "Every problem you have is constant." Problems
were always arising.

For example, the press raised an issue over a water shortage
in the city, creating disturbing headlines that New York City
would eventually use up its water supply. Mayor Wagner was
forced to call in experts to investigate pipe leakage and then
to create rain-making experiments. Bragdon believed these
were forced "upon us by the media." The mayor had to be
staged as "doing something" to alleviate the water shortage.

Paul Bragdon had the general responsibility of communicating with all media of the press, the public, and the
commissioners through press releases, speeches, and briefings.
Bragdon's responsibility was equal to that of the previous
press secretaries to Mayor Wagner, but his power and
influence were reduced due to the fact that he was a spokesman for a man who declined further mayoral service. Both
the mayor and his press secretary were lame ducks.

Jeffrey Roche had been a reporter on the *Journal-American*
who assumed the position of Assistant Executive Secretary
to Mayor Wagner in 1958.[10] He actually served as an assistant
press secretary, although in less than two years his official
title was changed to Director of Communications.

Roche claimed that job requirements of the press secretary
should include media experience, particularly with newspapers. It was not necessary to be the greatest writer in the
world, but the press secretary should know what an editor
wanted. It was equally essential that the press secretary be
totally loyal to the mayor.

The press secretary's responsibility included providing
information to the public. He also would get a sense of
public opinion from political leaders who would tell him
"what was cooking from both political parties." The press
chief had to maintain liaison with other public relations units
in all departments and with their commissioners. It had to be
made perfectly clear what the administration wanted and

coordinated information must be quickly disseminated to accomplish these ends.

Roche never saw himself as an advisor or counselor, but rather as being supportive to the mayoral administration. But Roche recognized that the press secretary should be involved in policy-making.

Certainly in the cabinet when discussing things the press secretary is free to utter his opinions. Sometimes his opinions influence a decision. It is the press secretary's job to read all the newspapers and see what's going on. Therefore the press secretary could have a better feel on a situation.[10]

The press chief's decisions affected the patterns of action throughout the mayor's organization.

Roche insisted that it was important for a mayor to have a press secretary. The mayor could not possibly answer every inquiry, and he, accordingly, should have an officer in authority to answer a question or to get an authentic qualification on an issue.

Someone has got to do it or there would be chaos. All the reporters in Room 9 can't all be going into the mayor's office every two seconds.

Our judgment is very important, particularly during night calls when the executive secretary must make the decision whether or not to call the mayor or the commissioner. The importance of the support of the executive secretary was demonstrated many times. For example, the Parks Commissioner had barred someone from speaking in Central Park. It became embarrassing to the mayor. It would have been advisable to have cleared this departmental action with the executive/press secretary. Sometimes people, regardless of their authority and responsibility, are not aware of what they are doing. They do not recognize that by ignoring the public they are getting the mayor and his entire administration into trouble.[10]

Another situation involved the traffic commissioner.

Some women wanted a traffic stop light put at a crossing. Engineering-wise it was not important. The women marched with prams and carriages and blocked traffic. They got their traffic light. Here, again, had the traffic commissioner been in communication with the executive secretary this public demonstration could have been avoided. A situation had been created by the demonstration for lack of doing something.

If I saw a bad story, I would handle it myself. Before I called the mayor, I would call the commissioner. I would get to the commissioner before the mayor even knew about it.[10]

Roche actually was the second man to the press secretary or the executive secretary. Many of the journalists working for the electronic media sought out Jeffrey Roche for his advice on the newsworthiness of a story, for they had very few correspondents who could be assigned to cover City Hall regularly.

They would call and ask if it were worthwhile for them to cover a story; where would the mayor be; should they bring down their equipment.[10]

The program "Direct Line" was begun during Mayor Wagner's administration over the National Broadcasting Network. The press secretary's office arranged who would be on the show and what the subject matter would be. People would phone in questions, which Roche emphasized, "We did not screen . . . although we were asked to." However,

If there were a lot of questions that were in the same vein, then it was up to our office to determine what questions to pursue, but there was no set up as far as we were concerned.[10]

The press office serving the mayor included an executive secretary and an assistant executive secretary. Warren Moscow was the speech writer, as well as a member of the mayor's cabinet. He also had direct liaison with the various departments.

The staff worked informally with the mayor. Both William Peer, as executive secretary, and Jeffrey Roche maintained direct contact with him.

Most of the time the relationship of Peer as press secretary to the mayor was informal, Roche had observed. If the press secretary wanted to see the mayor, he would say to the mayor's secretary "I would like to see the mayor as soon as I can." Occasionally he walked into the mayor's office. It would be rare that the press secretary would ever have to interrupt the mayor.

At least twice a week Roche met the mayor at Gracie Mansion and rode to City Hall with him, "and in the car I would go through the invitational mail with him. I would ask him 'do you want to send this letter?' 'Do you want to go to his place?' or what have you. The relationship with the mayor was both professional and personal. It's easier if you like the fellow and get along with him."[10]

Roche also worked closely with William Peer and Warren Moscow informally. Moscow would show his speeches to the press secretary or his assistant, and they would discuss it together.

Warren Moscow wrote all the speeches. He was very capable. We had to work together although he worked directly out of the mayor's office.[10]

Sometimes Roche would have a drink or lunch with a columnist (and often used the opportunity to launch a trial balloon). He also was on constant call with reporters in the evening:

By the time I got from the office to my home I would call my answering service; this I repeated every forty minutes. Once I got home I would tell the answering service to switch all calls over. I would answer calls immediately from any of the media. I would try so that they would have no more than a thirty to forty minute gap between the time they placed their call to me and my returning of the call. I gave as much service as possible to the media so as not to let any story get out of hand.

Sometimes we would get calls late at night and we could not make a decision. We would have to call Gracie Mansion, but the decision to call Gracie Mansion would be the press secretary's and not the reporter's.

Roche avoided controversy with the news media, and maintained a direct and warm relationship with most of the newspaper reporters. But that did not mean he backed away from reporters if they posed antagonistic questions or wrote articles unfavorable to the mayor. When asked how he felt when the press abused the mayor or himself, Roche replied, "That's part of the game. You sometimes have questions that trap you and you have to worry about it so that you don't make an idiot of yourself."[10]

Sometimes personal, political, and administrative quarrels were carried on through the press, particularly during campaign time.

If something was damaging in a story you wanted your version to get into the papers before too much time had elapsed. If the facts were erroneous the mayor had to take drastic action to counteract it.[10]

Although the press office was run without any rigid procedures, its functions were performed regularly. A daily schedule was issued to the press that listed public functions that were to take place at City Hall and public meetings the mayor was to attend. This public list was issued to the press at 5:00 a.m. every weekday. Newspapers could advise their reporters to seek further explanation and arrange for pictures. Some papers would check carefully to verify if the mayor were going to be present or merely intended to pay a token visit.

Bill Peer issued a release in the name of the mayor to cut down on ceremonies. This was editorially good, because it also reduced the load on newspapers and their reporters. Unfortunately the mayor was not able to keep his promise, because every cause in the city was a good cause and the pleading from the various organizations in the city was that we need you very badly, and the mayor would respond.[10]

A private list, including meetings of the mayor with the commissioners or others at Gracie Mansion also was drawn up with the help of the mayor's secretary. Stories had to be devised for the 6 o'clock televised news frequently, and televised press conferences with the mayor arranged. Quite often a press conference would be impromptu and held in the mayor's office. At other times, to accommodate the television crew, it would be held in the Blue Room opposite the mayor's office in City Hall.

I would call up a publisher of possibly the *Journal-American* or *Daily Mirror* and say to him, "I wonder if it would be possible for you to see Mayor Wagner and have a talk with him before you come out editorially." If a story was blatantly wrong, I might call up the editor or publisher to point this out. Most of the time we would get a fair reaction from the press.

We were not that formal in the holding of daily press conferences. Lindsay, I believe, scheduled one for every Friday. A newspaper would want a particular thing answered, so we might call a spontaneous press conference and get it on the item.[10]

When a reporter asked for an exclusive newspaper story, Jeffrey Roche maintained he would not give anyone anything more than anyone else. However, if an enterprising reporter came up with provocative information, "we would check out the story for him."

There might not be any press conferences for two or three days, but on other occasions three or four might be held in one day. (In addition to meeting the press at press conferences, the reporters could catch the mayor when he was walking in or out of his office and ask him questions.) The press secretary tried to give as much information to the reporters as he possibly could. He would resort to "no comment" infrequently and then mostly because he did not have a complete answer to the question that was posed.

In as equally an informal manner as press conferences were conducted, Roche would write letters to the editor, signing them in the name of the mayor, or even with the names of relatives of members of the office staff. These were used to gain support for an issue that did not warrant a press release or to counteract opposition in a noncontroversial manner.

Roche was of the opinion that the assistant press secretary should be the tactician who presented the policy the mayor wanted to the public, rather than serving as policy-maker himself. His job involved public relations primarily.

Timothy J. Cooney served as an assistant in the press secretary's office during Mayor Wagner's administration.[6] He distributed the press releases of the mayor and the city departments personally to the reporters in Room 9, after they had been cleared by the mayor.

When Debs Myers left City Hall, Leslie Slote became acting press secretary, and I became Leslie's assistant. Shortly after, Debs came back. Leslie never had the confidence of the mayor that Debs had. The mayor wanted Debs to come back, and he wanted things kept as tidy as possible.

What I developed for my role they had never had before. It was necessary for someone to go around with the mayor wherever he went and keep him on his way. My job, as we followed the mayor's public schedule was to hop out of the car, and talk to the newsmen. I would try to jolly them along so that we could get all the newsmen at one time to talk to the mayor. If this were not done, the mayor's public schedule was such that reporters and television station commentators would approach us individually on these scheduled stops and tease out the mayor's day. The mayor sort of became dependent on this approach. The reporters would sometimes be annoyed. Wagner said to them, "Don't pay any attention to him (Tim)," and meanwhile Wagner would say, "Jesus Christ," as one after another would individually try to pop a question to him. And my response would be, "You can only get to one reporter this way."

I went everywhere with the mayor. When the mayor was campaigning for Bob Kennedy, we were going virtually around the clock. A lot of little things came up on these stops. One woman approached me and said her husband had been in jail, and I would pass it on to the proper department.

I didn't need to be with the mayor in City Hall. At City Hall I would write all the messages, including the letters of congratulations. Those would collect on my desk. Leslie or Debs would look at them. They might take it up with the mayor or I might take it and take it up with the mayor in the car. I would ask him about what he wanted to do with them. In this manner it would have initial clearance. Bert Green, the secretary in the office, also screened these messages and the letters of congratulations which had to be written. She had a lot of power and sometimes made the decisions even before we got to it.

If a formal speech were necessary, we turned it over to Julius Edelstein, the mayor's speech writer. About one out of 50 requests for speeches by the mayor were accepted. Julius Edelstein reported directly to the mayor, although he worked with the press secretary's office.

Anything that came in on the day of an occasion received a telegram. This was automatic. We had a pool of secretaries working on this continuously. On the day of an occasion, when the mayor wouldn't go, I would dictate a message to the secretary relevant to the occasion. We would "tease out" something like that.

On one occasion I was in the office, and Mayor Wagner was at
lunch. We had just received the announcement that Governor
Stevenson had died. The key role I had was to write our statement
on the death ahead of anyone else. I had it typed up. Then I called
Debs Myers at lunch, and he made a few changes. Then I shot it
down to Room 9, and we made the afternoon papers. This meant
a great deal to the people involved.

There is one man in the city who will not speak to the mayor
today. I forgot to tell the mayor about the death of this man's
wife, and so the mayor never "sent" a letter of condolence.

The first thing the mayor read in the morning was the obituary
column. The formal letters of condolence the mayor wanted to send
out I would get over the phone. The mayor would call me in the
morning. Then the girls would type the letters carefully. The
messages and letters in the mayor's name were all signed by Gloria
Cipriano.

There were many interdepartmental problems. One basic administrative difficulty was that no one person knew in whose jurisdiction
substantive, final decisions lay. The press secretary's office often
sank into the melting of problems.

Unfortunately I didn't sink my teeth into the interdepartmental
problems as much as I would have liked to. This was particularly
so, because Edelstein was building a bigger empire for himself.
Edelstein was working twenty-four hours a day, and it was hard to
get around him. On the other hand those who worked for Edelstein
had a passion for anonymity. He tended to attract persons who did
not have strong personalities.[6]

Cooney's relationship with the press was friendly but he
did not regard the reporters in Room 9 very highly. "I
always thought Room 9 was the waste of manpower. In
order to give an announcement, you had to walk in to
Room 9 and they were of course always hanging around
waiting for you."[6]

Cooney believed that the reporters held the office of
press secretary in contempt as well, mainly because the
mayor undercut the office. For example, the television
reporters would always try to film the mayor outside of
City Hall. Cooney would tell the reporters that the mayor
was not in, but at the same instant the mayor would be
allowing the cameras to record him on even the most
trivial of affairs.

(Cooney could only conclude that the radio and television reporters moved more skillfully than did the newspaper reporters. They tended to do what the press would not: found out where the mayor actually was, and question him.)

Cooney had definite views on the office of the press secretary:

The main thing the city needs is to have those problems articulated, but no wise politician wants to do that. It snaps into isms that are frightening. Therefore a press secretary is reduced to the role of not aiding the city but of keeping the guy alive politically.

The mayor could easily afford to cut his press staff and handle mechanical problems with the press. I think the press is so important today in terms of bigger scale thinking. Public relations is a skill and then there must be someone to handle that skill. The public relations adviser in this day and age is really needed by the great man. The top adviser to the great man must be a man with great sense. He must know how to call up and deal with top people.

I finally got bored with the job. I thought I would have some input in some of the city's problems. I had been with the Commission of Human Rights and the Commission of Labor. I had found out that the last thing the mayor wanted was to hear my advice, but he liked me as a young kid who could call the press and talk sports with him . . . . it got to be tiresome with the mayor talking shop.[6]

Warren Moscow, who had originally been a *New York Times* reporter, had been with Mr. Wagner when Wagner served as Borough President of Manhattan from 1949 to 1953, and previously when Mr. Wagner had been City Commissioner of Housing and Buildings in 1947.[11]

Warren Moscow first assumed his post as Assistant to the Mayor in 1958 (in 1961 his title was changed to read "executive assistant to the mayor"). He was directly responsible for writing speeches and some press releases that he would take up to the mayor for approval. He and the press secretary prepared the mayor for a press conference.

Doyle and I would shoot all the questions and frame the answers. He would act as the devil's advocate.[11]

The relationship between Warren Moscow and the mayor
was pleasant. He was a trusted friend of Mayor Wagner. In
addition, he was an intellectual, and the mayor admired his
thinking and his integrity. Very frequently the press secretary and Moscow would meet the mayor for breakfast
and often would ride down to City Hall with him.

The biggest problem Warren Moscow and others in the
mayor's office had to deal with concerned Julius Edelstein,
another mayoral assistant and speech writer, who was to
succeed Mr. Moscow. Edelstein had difficulty responding
to press deadlines and communicating with others in the
office. In addition, Edelstein sometimes would decide
policy while writing a speech for the mayor without discussing the speech with the press secretary's office. Edelstein posed a problem, because he would not coordinate
his responsibilities with the press secretary's office or other
mayoral assistants.

William Peer and Debs Myers had a great opportunity to
serve the mayor intimately, for Wagner even allowed them
to share his inner self up to a point. Both served, as well,
as policy makers and advisors to the mayor. Emanuel
Perlmutter of the *New York Times* maintained that the
first press secretary who exercised political power was Debs
Myers. "The status was in policymaking."[12] Debs Myers
always seemed to be doing the right thing. He had a lack
of cynicism and a sense of realism. The difference in the
mayor's attitude may be explained in terms of the degree
to which he trusted his press secretaries.

Frank Doyle, according to observers, never really was
an intimate press secretary to the mayor. Warren Moscow
really carried on that function. Doyle did not have the
sparkle and the scope to move in a commanding executive
capacity, nor did he have the ability to write. Frank Doyle's
performance was mechanical, prosaic, and uninspiring.
Leslie Slote never had that confidence of the mayor nor
the association that Debs Myers had experienced. Leslie
Slote served the mayor as a strong *technical* press secretary,

not as a confidante with broad-ranging opportunities.

Paul Bragdon was an interim appointee who succeeded Leslie Slote, and he also served during the last months of the Wagner administration as a technical press secretary. Although he sat in on many cabinet and other meetings the mayor had arranged, his responsibilities basically involved writing, arranging, scheduling, and distributing news.

NINE

JOHN V. LINDSAY

John Lindsay was elected mayor of New York City as a
Republican in November 1965. He won reelection in
November 1969 on the Liberal Party ticket, having lost the
Republican primary election that summer.

During his tenure, Mayor Lindsay had three press secretaries; each has differed in personality and in the manner
in which he discharged the secretary's responsibilities.

Woody Klein was a reporter for the *New York World-
Telegram,* specializing in housing during the time he helped
elect Lindsay. For his efforts he was offered a job in the
city administration by Robert Price (the campaign manager
and soon to be Deputy Mayor):

I told him I was not certain I wanted to run a city agency but
rather if I did come into the administration I wanted to do something related to journalism. We talked about the job of press
secretary. I told him I might be interested. . . .

Harry O'Donnell who had been Lindsay's press aide during the
campaign was rumored for the job. . . . However, Harry O'Donnell
had never gotten along well with Bob Price because Bob Price would
never check with him before leaking stories to newsmen. As a
result there were reports that O'Donnell did not want to work for

Lindsay if Price did, and during this time Lindsay was publicly
trying to persuade Price to be his deputy mayor.[1]

Woody Klein accepted the position of press secretary,
but it was to be a difficult ten and a half months that he
served. Bob Price, as Deputy Mayor, continued to release
stories to newsmen without consulting Klein.

Bob Price had run a highly successful campaign by fully utilizing
the fine art of leaking stories, one here, another there, making sure
every reporter got one exclusive, and there was little doubt that it
was Price who was giving out many of the stories ahead of time.
This did not make my job any easier at the outset. Finally, one day
in mid-December, one newspaper carried a "dope" story about how
Lindsay was considering "dumping" Vincent P. Broderick as Police
Commissioner, because he [Broderick] was not in favor of the
Civilian Review Board Lindsay had pledged to create in his campaign. Lindsay telephoned me from his suite—Room 861—as soon as
he saw the newspaper.

"Woody, can you find out who leaked that story about Broderick?
There's not a word of truth to it. Issue a denial immediately in my
name, will you?"

I wasted no time in heading for Bob Price's office next to
Lindsay's. I went in and told him of my conversation with Lindsay.

"Look here," Price said sternly. "Are you accusing me of
leaking that story?"

"I'm not accusing you of anything. I just want to know if you
have any idea who might have done it?"

"I don't have to tell you what I do. I don't have to tell Lindsay,
either. I know what's best for him—I know what is better for him
that he does. Now I don't want to talk about this any more." He
turned his back and answered one of the three telephones that were
ringing on his desk.

The next day I arranged to have lunch with the reporter who had
written the story about Broderick. I told him what had happened
and then explained to him that even though I knew better than to
ask a newsman who his source was, the Mayor-elect wanted to
know. I asked him point-blank who had given him the Broderick
lead.

"Look," he said, "you know I can't tell you officially. But this
much I can say. Your instincts are right. You're going to have
trouble from that other fellow after you get to City Hall. That's
why Harry O'Donnell didn't want to stay on with Lindsay as press

secretary and that's why you're going to have a rough time." The
reporter and I both knew we were talking about Bob Price.[1]

Klein had definite ideas concerning the qualifications
of the press secretary:

It is advisable for a press secretary to have had a journalism career
and some professionalization in the news media of one form or another.
It helps to have been a news reporter at the working level. At the
other side of the fence you know what are the demands of truth in
politics. The dedicated newspaperman believes there is one truth.
In politics you've got to get the guy with less than the truth. The
man must know how to manipulate the language. The press secretary
has to be a skilled manipulator. . . .
Make your mind up that you are going to live in a fish bowl.
Establish yourself as early as possible as an administrator that is
going to take risks. Have access to your executive as often as possible
and personally as a group. Hold background briefings for the press
not as "attributable stuff"; even though the press is organically an
adversary, they should be made to feel close to the operation.
Reporters have to be part of the operation even though there are
personality problems that do arise within any system. . . .
There is a constant struggle as to who has the upper hand, the
press secretary or the press. They want that power and want to
exercise it. It is a continuing battle in a democratic government.
On the other hand it is an essential battle to keep the fibers of
government continuously glistening. . . .
The reporters don't want to be held at arms length. You've got to
always be ready for the unexpected; the unannounced, the
embarrassing things; it takes three men to be on top of such things. . . .
At the outset I tried to impose arbitrary announcements that the
mayor was making without allowing questions and answers. I tried to
hold press conferences. I tried to get the written press in separately.[2]

Mayor's Lindsay's press conferences were scheduled
twice a week, on Tuesdays and Fridays. The mayor was
briefed on probable topics just before a press conference
was to begin. Sometimes other assistants and municipal
executives attended these briefings. At other times the
mayor might be briefed in the car as he and Klein were
driven to City Hall. The meetings were opened by Klein
with a few statements or announcements, and the conferences usually lasted thirty to forty-five minutes.

In the beginning at a joint press conference we had the Room 9 press
corps and the television crew in with the mayor every six to eight
weeks. We were experimenting the first weeks. We established sort
of exclusive interviews with the Room 9 reporters on a non-direct
quote basis; the "mayor feels" concept. We set up those kinds of
interviews. Twenty to thirty people from one day to the next would
be covering the mayor in any one twelve-hour cycle. No public
figure can survive without some kind of news secretary.[2]

Part of the task was to think about the public and how to
serve the public while serving the mayor.

Klein also tried to establish procedures for dealing with
the press.

I maintained that one should be forthright and frank. I wasn't much
on frills. I wasn't much on trial balloons. I became press secretary
giving out facts. Backgrounders I didn't give. I wasn't versatile
for that.

Harry O'Donnell was a master in entertaining the press and of
dropping hints and suggesting stories without laying it on the line.
He was able to steer the mayor much more professionally.[2]

Woody Klein took a serious view of the ways he had to
deal with the press because of the demands he felt his
position imposed.

Everything he [the mayor] did was my daily work. I was addressing
myself to how he was seen. Everything he did became my concern;
it was all-consuming. I lost track of my personal life; there were
phones in my bedroom; my wife never got any sleep. I couldn't go
anywhere without calling anyone. I would call my answering service
from a road stand. I would have to be available twenty-four hours a
day, seven days a week. The mayor was always available; he never
got any rest. I had to get to the office before him and leave after
him.[2]

Klein felt that he was more than an executive assistant
to the mayor. He attended the regular staff meetings:

At this time, Lindsay was moving ahead with additional municipal
financial belt-tightening, which was guaranteed to make more news.
"I attended his [the mayor's] regular Tuesday morning staff meetings
at 8 A.M. with his two deputy mayors, aides Gene Becker, Lee
Rankin, Bob Sweet, and a few others. . . .

All good administration in the world is not going to help the mayor unless he simultaneously is getting sound political counsel. The press secretary should be playing a role in the counseling. If he happens to be only good at being a technical man, he should still be in on sessions, and approve of what is happening.

"You cannot inhibit your executive. There is a very delicate balance," Klein maintained, "in meeting the needs of the political executive, and meeting the needs of the press."

You've got to be a middle man and honest broker. You have to develop a position where both the press and your boss are willing to listen to you. You may not be the greatest practitioner, but you keep the flow of information going in and out, and you keep it honestly. The press secretary can't know everything that is happening. The guy needs a little room, a little elbow.

The press secretary has got to know how to feed the news to reporters. You've got to feed trial balloons. They want a story between the media and the politician. The politician only exists on what the media says he is doing. It's not necessarily what the mayor is doing; it is in theory trying to make it fit into what the press says he is doing.

If you have a chief executive who is not very strong, then you need a strong press secretary. Lindsay in the beginning was not a strong mayor. Lindsay on the other hand had a strong deputy mayor and a straight press secretary. The deputy mayor was carrying a political role. Deputy Mayor Sweet was a straight guy. Harry O'Donnell became a strong press secretary. When you have Dick Aurelio as deputy mayor who was also a very strong political administrator, then you have in a sense Tom Morgan as a straight press secretary. I became more of a straight spokesman.

You've got to be ruthless to be a successful politician. Lindsay seemed to depend on a strong deputy mayor. The chief executive is always shifting his teams around. He keeps shifting, but he is still there. To be a press man in that situation is rough. Anything less than what you promise is going to fail.[2]

John Lindsay had said, "I hope we can keep the press fat, satisfied and comfortable." But, with Woody Klein, the press had been uncomfortable, for there had been many conflicts with Price, leaks, and press conferences that had left many unanswered questions.[3]

Klein missed his newspaper work, and he felt he had been a misfit in his job mainly because he had not complemented his chief executive. He had instead been as idealistic and sensitive as the mayor.

And so in ten and one half months I had answered thousands of inquiries from the press, put out 460 press releases, and acted as the mayor's spokesman on many occasions. Yet for me and for many others close to the mayor, it had been a nerve-racking experience which had left us drained and weary. I felt completely spent. I had struggled, along with Lindsay, against what now seemed to be overwhelming odds. Lindsay's image had been severely tarnished. I had tried my best and yet the whole year had turned out to be disappointing and painful. It seemed like the end of a nightmare. And now that it was coming to a close, I knew that the change would be 'best for the mayor and, even more important, best for me and my family.[3]

Harry O'Donnell had been a member of the Associated Press, covering the State Legislature in Albany. He also had served Governor Dewey for two years and then the Republican State Committee to cover eleven state campaigns. After the 1965 Lindsay campaign O'Donnell went back to Albany, but in 1966 he was asked to succeed Woody Klein as press secretary to the mayor.[4]

O'Donnell had definite ideas concerning the requirements of the office of the press secretary to the mayor:

The press secretary has to have a know-how; he has to have ability to execute and to articulate without putting his foot into his mouth.

By the very nature of the role, the more effective press secretary is one that has an intimate personal relationship with his principal. Further, a press secretary should be a professional rather than an ideologist. He should be a generalist in his broad knowledge and have common sense, particularly in his use of communications.[4]

O'Donnell stated that the press secretary to the mayor had several important functions to perform:

One is responsible to the public—keeping the public continuously and correctly informed about the actions of the mayor.[4]

This he accomplished chiefly through the news media. The second was responsibility *to* the news media: to make it easier and more convenient for the reporter to do a good job. A reporter might call the press secretary to ask what was the best news in the story or "What's the lead you would like us to have for the story?" Tom O'Hara of the *New York Herald Tribune* often would do this.

It is to your advantage to tell him. Basically the lead whould be in the last paragraph of the story. You ought to be honest, Mr. O'Donnell said, it's the political thing to do. Reporters have more respect for you and depend on you in a pinch. This way you prevent your reporter from looking bad. In addition news media wouldn't begin to do a comprehensive job without professional public relations. The press couldn't begin to cover government.

Room 9 has at the most ten to eleven guys, which include two or three from the *Times,* three or four from the *Daily News.* You need press people to be kept advised on things that are coming up. If a story is not written right, it is possible the press secretary did not give the reporter all of the material and explain to him all the angles. This is highly essential and indispensable for creating a good press job.[4]

The third was to serve the mayor as efficiently as possible. O'Donnell also felt the press secretary should participate in policy-making and advise the mayor on matters related to the city and his own political career. For example, he suggested to Mayor Lindsay that he take Robert Kennedy's Senate seat, which it was rumored was to be offered after the Senator's assassination.

He was consulted on everything from the strategy for battling Representative Paul Fino, the anti-Lindsay Bronx Republican leader; to policy for the Department of Water Supply, Gas and Electricity. "Harry is as close to me as any member of the team. I haven't a thought about the city that he doesn't know," the mayor said.

He had been a softening influence on the mayor. Gone are such arrogant and self-righteous pre-O'Donnell Lindsayisms as: "If I am frustrated, it is the people who will be the losers." O'Donnell had taught the mayor to suffer his critics with tolerance and even amusement; at least in public.

The O'Donnell touch was also applied to the little courtesies that oil the machinery of municipal government and politics. The first day that O'Donnell took office he showed his style. Lindsay and his young men, including Klein, had by then alienated every Democrat in City Hall. It was the day that Marine Sgt. Robert E. O'Malley was returning home to Queens after receiving the Medal of Honor. The mayor was leaving City Hall to meet O'Malley at the airport.

"Look," said O'Donnell to the mayor, "O'Connor's from Queens. Why don't we take him with us? City Council President Frank D. O'Connor is the municipal government's highest-ranking Democrat.[1] It was the kind of courtesy in which Lindsay aides had been so notably lacking, and it paid off. For days after, O'Connor had nothing but good things to say about the mayor.

O'Donnell loved the minutiae of politics and government almost as much as he loved the sweet crack of a New York Yankee line drive.[5]

O'Donnell served as press secretary with two assistant press secretaries, an office administrator, a stenographer, receptionist, and a college intern (there also was a speech writer who worked directly with the mayor). He also relied on the press officers of the various city departments.

The press secretary in order to anticipate questions and happenings, scheduled his own briefings to be informed as to what the departments and the commissioners were doing. He would first call the information officer of the department and would ask him to put down some questions. The mayor's press secretary might ask the commissioner to come to the press secretary's briefing to explain the various aspects of the situation.[4]

Although most press releases were cleared by the departments themselves, special items were sent to the mayor for final approval before the press secretary had them distributed.

Sometimes press releases were issued as "overnights" that is, news items due to be released for morning papers were distributed the night before so that the editors would have plenty of time to include them in the morning editions. At other times stories were leaked to reporters, but O'Donnell tried to prevent any one reporter from uncovering a scoop on City Hall from sources outside his own office. (Every now and then, however, he did give a reporter a confidential story, but would require that the reporter keep quiet about it, thereby avoiding a scoop he otherwise might have made.)

O'Donnell arranged interviews for the mayor with the
editors of newspapers and magazines, such as those of the
Wall Street Journal and *U. S. News and World Report.* He
also scheduled the mayor to appear on television, for interviews with Johnny Carson among others.

Our motive was to go and transmit the personality we had in John
Lindsay. He would get one serious fact across and humor.[4]

O'Donnell carefully briefed the mayor before these
interviews so much so that an editor of *U. S. News* said of
John Lindsay, "that's the kind of man the Republicans
ought to run for President." The mayor was successful
with his television appearances, as well, because O'Donnell
was careful to have him appear only when the mayor had
something to say. O'Donnell felt a public official should
say how he wanted things, but the press secretary should
suggest the time when the mayor should say it. The press
secretary had to be careful that anything the mayor said was
not quoted out of context, but even more difficult to overcome was the fact that everything the mayor might say on
television would be heard by the public immediately.
There was no room for evasion. The mayor, however, did
not have these problems with his own television show,
presented on WNEW-TV from November 1967 to January
1972. The mayor was carefully advised by David Garth,
an outside consultant who worked with the press secretary.

O'Donnell held press conferences that were as carefully
planned as the mayor's television program. The press secretary could prepare beforehand a question that was current,
and, after he had determined how the mayor would answer,
he could handily produce the appropriate response for the
reporters. Also, O'Donnell could steer the line of questioning to benefit the mayor during a conference with reporters.

In addition to preparing news releases and scheduling
interviews for the mayor. Harry O'Donnell arranged for
press coverage of some of Lindsay's famous "walks," for
example, the night Martin Luther King died, when O'Donnell
and Dave Garth walked through Harlem together with the

mayor. As a demonstration of sympathy and an act of
courage, it was well received by Harlem residents as well as
the rest of the city. On another occasion the press secretary
scheduled coverage when the mayor and Christian Herter, a
former member of the President's cabinet, toured on foot
some of New York's slums. It produced a good press,
especially on television and radio.

Harry O'Donnell usually enjoyed a good relationship with
the press, and even those who did not like him thought he
was not "all bad." O'Donnell had seen the press secretary's
office as essential to the people's right to know, and he
considered it important to help the reporters gather the
news as well. He also enjoyed the respect and trust of
Mayor Lindsay. O'Donnell quit his job as press secretary
only when it became apparent to him that Mayor Lindsay
would run for reelection as a fusion candidate on the
Liberal ticket—Harry O'Donnell had been a lifelong Republican and he could not further serve the mayor without com-
promising his basic party loyalty.

Thomas B. Morgan succeeded Harry O'Donnell as press
secretary to Mayor Lindsay. Earlier he had been a press
aide to Adlai Stevenson during Stevenson's unsuccessful
campaign for the 1960 Democratic presidential nomination.
He also had worked as a free-lance writer for *Life, Look,*
and *Esquire.* "I consider myself pretty much of a literary
person and journalist."[6] He also had worked, along with
other journalists and Mayor Lindsay, on the Koerner Commission civil rights presidential report.

Robert Laird worked for Morgan as the Assistant Press
Secretary; he had been hired by Woody Klein in 1966 after
working with him on the *New York World-Telegram.* Laird
and Morgan worked in a huge office with several assistants.
It included having an assistant sponsored by the Sloan
Foundation Urban Fellowship Program. One of the press
aides was responsible for liaison with neighborhood and
ethnic newspapers. The neighborhood press office has been

in operation since November 1969 and employs two full-
time people and one part-time, as well as two volunteers.
It produces press releases concerning neighborhood events.
The speech writers also worked under Morgan's jurisdiction,
although their office was separate from the press secretary's
staff. The speechwriters would make a draft of a speech for
the mayor and then consult with him, Deputy Mayor
Aurelio, and staff man, Jay Kriegel. Then Morgan would
read the speech, and his own staff would then rewrite it.
Laird would write the related press releases.

Morgan maintained contact with the press officers of
each of the city agencies and especially with Jay Kriegel,
who served as the major liaison officer, head of the mayor's
executive staff, and the man who monitored all of the city
employees. Morgan had the responsibility of determining
whether or not an individual should be hired as a departmental press secretary and approved the starting salaries.
He emphasized, however, that "I defer to the commissioner
unless I think the mistake of appointing a man is horren-
dous." He thus had a great influence on the public relations
of the city departments.

In addition they don't make statements or hold press conferences
without checking with me. They do in effect clear with me their
major movement. However the relationship is circular, in a sense
that the commissioner or public relations man might call me. However
the general staff liaison again is Jay Kriegel. I don't necessarily get
in touch with these people, but they must contact Jay Kriegel and
we might then develop this circular motion. On the other hand, if
I don't like something the PR guy has stated, I will make the change.[6]

Mr. Laird commented:

We are in a sense at the tip of the pyramid. In a loose sense all of
the department press secretaries are (sic) responsible to us. If
there is some snafu the buck stops with us and we chastise the press
officer involved. To avert conflict an agency tells us when they are
planning to do something . . .
This is not a rigid relationship. A commissioner or administrator
could be calling up and talking to the press officer any time he
wanted to. The agency press officer would call to talk to either Tom

Morgan or Bob Laird, particularly if another department wishes to
make an announcement involving the mayor. The commissioner may
want to announce a particular happening but it may really be a
mayoral announcement...

Mayor Lindsay wants to be involved in all activities, but the
mayor cannot always be held accountable. The commissioner's
office may drop the release if we would announce it.[7]

Morgan also worked closely with the deputy mayor, Richard
Aurelio, who kept up with every detail of the operation of
the city.

The deputy mayor was the next most powerful man in
city government after the mayor, and he supervised all of
the press secretary's operations, although he often would
suggest that Morgan clear important press releases with
Jay Kriegel. Morgan, accordingly, considered the "third
most important job in the Lindsay administration is the
press job." He also felt he had substantial influence
serving as the mayor's spokesman. Actually, the office
was almost a separate administrative group of the mayor's
office.

The press secretary floats between the deputy mayor and the mayor.
The press secretary's operation is an extension of the mayor; Mr.
Morgan has seen it as a partner with the deputy mayor.[7]

Morgan commented that "nobody thinks to separate the
press secretary from the mayor."

Morgan thought the press secretary primarily should be a
journalist and less of an administrator and that the press
secretary's office should not be run rigidly, because news
stories often develop rapidly, and decisions on what should
be issued to the press had to be made quickly and by someone experienced in dealing with the news. The office could
not afford the time to clear statements through the
bureaucracy. Above all, the press secretary had to appear
credible to newsmen.

The judgment factor in credibility is essential to the job. Of course
the question is relative, who is to say what is good judgment. You
never know from day to day....

I have never lied, and I have only once said something to the press
that wasn't true; but I didn't know it; someone had given me bad
information. In this you have the mobility of the bureaucracy. If
there are any threats to the credibility of the mayor and myself,
myself being a spokesman for the mayor, it then makes the position
less than tenable. The politician press secretary is a dangerous
game to play.[6]

The major responsibility of the press secretary was to
issue press releases of statements made by the mayor, for
which reason Laird considered the press office as a service
function primarily. The mayor preferred to submit all of
his statements to the press in writing to maintain exact
control of the language and to avoid sloppiness. Often the
press secretary's office would write a statement on behalf
of the mayor and release it without consulting with the
mayor. Also the various city agencies might draft a
statement, but these were sent to the press secretary for
approval before they were released. Morgan also had to
brief the mayor for his television shows. He decided, with
Aurelio and others, what invitations the mayor should
accept to make speeches. The press secretary also handled
the mayor's correspondence and issued "letters to the
editor." To help him fulfill his responsibilities successfully,
Morgan constantly read the national and neighborhood
newspapers and magazines, and a staff member watched the
evening television news and wrote a summary of what was
reported.

Of course, Morgan always had to deal with the press.
Usually, there always were about a dozen reporters in Room
9, especially from the *New York Times* and the Associated
Press, who could see the mayor easily. The press secretary
saw to it that the reporters did not waste the mayor's time
by asking him to answer the same question more than once.
Sometimes Morgan or his assistant would go into Room 9
and chat with reporters. They might pass out releases and
tell the reporters if a major story was going to break. They
also would provide background material for news stories,
usually to the *New York Times,* if it was requested. Or,

reporters would come into the press secretary's office:

If a reporter comes to us and he was working on something exclusively, we protect him and answer him. . . .
    If a news reporter comes into the press secretary's office to ask about a rumor or a speculation the assistant press secretary may check it out to determine if there are feelers out on the situation.[6]

For instance, George Douris, reporter on the *Long Island Press* once questioned Laird, "anything to the fact that Al Lowenstein[8] is being considered for a job in the mayor's office?"

Laird immediately said, "I haven't heard about it, but I'll check it with Dick Aurelio and Ronnie Eldridge." (Mrs. Eldridge was a reform Democrat who had organized 'the "Democrats for Lindsay" and now was a member of the mayor's staff.) Laird left his own office and went into Aurelio's where Eldridge had been conferring with him. Laird then returned and said to Douris that there was nothing at the moment about Lowenstein. Douris then asked, "Can I say that the Administration is thinking about it?" and repeated that question several times. That seemed logical to Laird; the story was printed the next day that the Lindsay administration was considering Lowenstein "for a not as yet defined job." (In the end Lowenstein did *not* receive a job or an appointment in the Lindsay administration.)

Mr. Morgan conducted the press conferences with the mayor. He, Jay Kriegel, Deputy Mayor Aurelio, and staff aides would brief the mayor about half an hour before the conference and try to anticipate the questions that might be posed and draw up the answers for the mayor. Then Morgan would open the press conference with various announcements and after that indicate the mayor was ready for the reporters' questions. The mayor also held interviews with each City Hall reporter at the end of each year to discuss the triumphs and failures of the past year and to venture predictions for the coming year. By 1971 the interviews had become so time-consuming that he decided

to hold three separate conferences, one with the reporters
of the newspapers, then one with reporters for radio, and
then television stations.

Once every two weeks the mayor would have lunch with
a reporter, a policy which Morgan had started. When a
columnist arrived from out of town, Morgan would arrange
to "stick him in a car" with the mayor.

Despite Laird's consideration that the press secretary
primarily provided a service to the mayor in dealing with the
press, the secretary was involved in policy-making.

We are drawn into the budget operation; we attend the budget
meetings; the press secretary office gathers a lot of information
which is rather useful in other policymaking activity. . . .

The nature of the job warrants that Jay Kriegel, another high
level mayoral staff aide, and I must have total access to the mayor.
We talk to each other to bring problems to proper solutions. Our
gain is brain, commonsense, credibility, and total loyalty.[7]

Morgan was indeed involved in policy-making, but he
insisted:

I am not a professional politician. Aurelio performs this, which I
think is proper. I give my opinion, but I don't feel that my opinion
must be followed. There's got to be conflict between the com-
municator's role and the politician's role. If you try to do both you
do it at your own peril.[6]

In general, Morgan felt that his biggest problem had been
dealing with the large volume of news that Mayor Lindsay
generated, and he thought that the role of the press
secretary had become more complicated and more important
over the last ten years, principally because of television.
In spite of the increased work load, he did find the time to
overcome the poor press relations the Lindsay administration
had suffered under his predecessors. Morgan had concentrat-
ed on being a press secretary and less an advisor, although
he had a keen sense of the political environment. He clearly
defined the duties of his office, thereby avoiding many
organizational challenges and made every effort to fulfill
them successfully. He was a good tactical press secretary.

TEN

THE PRESS SECRETARY
AND THE WORKING PRESS

Joe Breu, a reporter for UPI who covered City Hall, expressed his opinions of those who have served as press secretaries to the mayors of New York City during an interview in March 1971. He respected the abilities of William Peer, Debs Myers, Leslie Slote, Paul Bragdon, and Harry O'Donnell. Breu thought that many people considered that Frank Doyle and Woody Klein were not very competent as press secretaries.[1]

Richard Reeves, of the *New York Times* also was interviewed in March 1971, and he felt that Tom Morgan was exceptionally capable as press secretary. However, he thought Morgan was more of an intellectual man and, on occasion, was not completely informed of events taking place around City Hall. As a result, he gave reporters incorrect information, although inadvertently. Reeves thought that this hurt Morgan's career, because reporters felt that the secretary might be lying, and his credibility, so necessary to presenting the mayor's programs and image convincingly, was suspect.

When you get bad information they are in trouble. You often do get bad information from the press secretary; that is because he is inept or he underrates the reporter. Press secretaries always try to convince reporters they are good. They will sometimes drop unfavorable information to retain their credibility.[2]

Reeves also made a definite evaluation of others who had served as press secretary in City Hall.

Harry O'Donnell was a professional; Woody Klein was an amateur. The professional would brief the executive on what the press was going to ask; he would know what is in the press' mind. . . . He doesn't let underlings release news. Woody Klein never visioned what he was doing. Harry O'Donnell introduced the way the mayor would respond in a press conference. O'Donnell might make a statement and then say "no questions" and the press would have to respect that.[2]

Gabe Pressman, a television news reporter in New York City, also was interviewed in March of 1971. He expressed the opinion that William Donoghue was the best press secretary to serve the mayors of New York. He felt Donoghue had a strong and commanding personality and was capable of averting the embarrassment Mayor O'Dwyer was constantly risking from his habit of making compulsive statements. Others he did not admire so much:

Frank Doyle was completely useless. He was helpless to the press secretary concept. Leslie Slote was embarrassing. Harry O'Donnell was a policy advisor more than anyone else.

Of course, these reporters also stated definite opinions concerning the stature of the office of the press secretary to the mayor. Reeves had a low opinion of press secretaries, despite his admiration of a few individuals:

I certainly don't think the job is the highlight of any reporter's career. I always considered it as a step down or a new career. To me a press secretary is a lying politician, not a social commentator.[2]

Reeves stated that "He would rather be remembered as a good reporter."

Joe Breu, the UPI reporter, had less definite feelings concerning the status of the press secretary. On the one hand,

To me, if a reporter is offered a press secretary's job, it is for him the highest kind of ambition. My suspicion is if you would offer the job to any reporter he would take it . . . really grab it. There is an excitement to it. It's a climax to one's self in a sense.[1]

On the other hand Breu felt the office was not so attractive because:

The press secretary job in the mayor's office was to be considered a dead-end job, but I don't know. Starting with Debs, the nature of the job changed.[1]

Certainly the press secretary to the mayor of New York City holds a transitory position, serving only as long as the mayor remains in office or as long as the mayor wants the secretary to remain.

Although some reporters held the office of the press secretary to the mayor in low esteem, they did feel a press secretary should fulfill certain demands that were often difficult to meet in order to succeed. As I have mentioned above, Richard Reeves, as do other reporters, felt that the secretary must be honest with them. The press secretary also should establish friendly relations with the press. As Breu recalled,

Relationships with reporters and the press secretary is essential; a personal relationship is even better. He can talk to a guy and alter a story. Debs had no hesitation in calling an editor to complain about a reporter—the way he wrote a story, how it was played up or a headline was written. *World Telegram, Journal American* editors received many phone calls from Debs. He had no hesitation in calling an editor if he felt something was not fair. Often the personal relationship between the press secretary and the reporters would have an influence on the story.[1]

Above all, the press secretary must serve the mayor. Richard Reeves stated:

The press secretary person has got to understand what it is the government of New York City has to get across to the public; what information they have to have. That has been an administrative function . . . What programs will be accepted by the public; what program should they pursue; the press secretary has a responsibility in enduring all of this. However the most important aspect of his job from his viewpoint is in serving his boss, which is different than in serving the public.

The specifics of the job have been to make the mayor look good, sell them his program, and get his viewpoint across effectively as possible.[2]

Emmanuel Perlmutter suggested during a phone conversation in March 1971 that the successful press secretary should not only present the mayor and his programs favorably, but also should serve as his advisor before either the mayor or his programs are presented to the public. A "press secretary should respond as a consultant to the mayor; he should be used in policy questioning—no one makes policy but the mayor, but the mayor should use his press secretary's counsel if he is good." And in order to provide counsel to the mayor, Perlmutter pointed out that the press secretary should be capable of selecting from all the events that have taken place, those that are relevant to a particular problem and present only those to the mayor. To do this, in turn, the press secretary must learn of all the events that are taking place around the city. The press secretary has to be able to persuade, to become involved in certain things he has no feelings about. As Harry O'Donnell had pointed out, "The missimplification of the press secretary office was the thought that you are simply getting your boss into the papers."[4]

As we have seen, the responsibilities of the press secretary to the mayor of New York City have increased and become more demanding over the years as the mayor's responsibilities have also become more complex and as the means of gathering and reporting the news have become more sophisticated. At first, Mayor Van Wyck and Mayor Seth Low could easily release news stories to the press themselves, as did Mayor McClellan very successfully, who had once been a journalist himself. Mayor Gaynor was the first mayor of New York City to rely on his executive secretary to release his speeches to the press. He, however, did submit his own letters to the editor. Mayor Mitchel reverted to the policy of acting as his own press secretary and carefully composed his speeches so that the entire text could easily be set up and printed. Mayor Hylan relied completely on the news staff of William Randolph Hearst, his major political supporter, to prepare his news releases. He did have a secretary who dealt with the press, but the secretary had been a former Hearst reporter. Then James Walker was elected mayor, and he relied on his wit and flair to provide stories for reporters himself and especially photographs. He used the press to convey his frolicsome life much more than his policies. Mayor LaGuardia was equally as colorful as Mayor Walker, in his own way, and he also acted as his own press secretary. He addressed himself especially to the newspapers published for the barely educated and acted as a radio commentator, immortalizing himself for reading the Sunday comics on the air. He did assign an assistant as a press functionary from time to time to administer routine chores for the press. All of these mayors, however, relied primarily on their own skills and personalities to generate press coverage for themselves.

William J. Donoghue became the first press secretary to a mayor of New York City as we understand that function today. He had been a newspaperman before he served Mayors O'Dwyer and Impelliteri. Accordingly, he was knowledgeable about his job, and the press respected him for his ability and honesty. Donoghue was primarily occupied with the duty of serving as a buffer between the working press and the mayor; he was not involved in policy-making decision, as later press secretaries would be.

Mayor Wagner continued to rely on a press secretary, changing the title of that office in 1965 from Executive Secretary to the Mayor, to Press Secretary to the Mayor. Frank Doyle was Mayor Wagner's first press secretary, but he commanded little respect either from the press or the mayor. William Peer was not much more successful during his tenure as press secretary, although he, as a press secretary, for the first time became involved with determining policy. The prestige and influence of the press secretary finally were established by Debs Myers who succeeded Peer. He not only was extremely skillful in dealing with the press, but his abilities were respected by the mayor and he was much involved not only with making decisions concerning policy, but in making commanding phone calls to commissioners, as well as reporters. As Emmanuel Perlmutter commented, Myers was the "first press secretary who had power"; whose "status was in policy-making."

Leslie Slote had worked for Debs Myers before he succeeded him as press secretary to Mayor Wagner. During the time he served in City Hall, his office lost some of the stature Myers had gained for it, because Slote was content to deal with deadlines and the other mechanics of journalism. He did not become intimate with the mayor, nor did he participate in policy-making. For that matter, he did not have a close working relationship with reporters either.

Paul Bragdon was named press secretary after Leslie Slote. He could not restore much more prestige or power to the office of press secretary than did Mr. Slote, mainly because he served with what amounted to an interim appointment until Mayor Wagner's final term was to run out. He did not have much influence on the news reported about City Hall, although Mayor Wagner had him contribute to the formulation of policy.

John Lindsay was elected mayor of New York City after Wagner had decided not to run again. He first selected Woody Klein for his press secretary, but, unfortunately Klein was an idealist who allowed his personal philosophy to interfere with his responsibilities. He created havoc with the mayor's press relations. Harry O'Donnell was appointed to succeed Klein, and he managed to regain the prestige and respect for his office that had been lost over the years since Debs Myers had served at City Hall. O'Donnell had been a professional journalist, and he was respected by newsmen and politicians alike. He became intimate with the mayor and enjoyed his trust. Accordingly, O'Donnell was closely involved in the decisions concerning Mayor Lindsay's programs as well as in the procedure for announcing them in the best possible light to assure acceptance by the public.

Mayor Lindsay next appointed Thomas Morgan to be his press secretary, and he has shown the qualifications and has met all of the responsibilities the position of press secretary to the mayor currently entails. Morgan has the technical journalistic background, ability, and integrity to deal with the representatives of the news media and to present the mayor in the best possible light. The reporters trust him in return. He has jurisdiction over the appointments of press secretaries for the various city departments and has control over distribution of the material they pass on to the press. Mr. Morgan is loyal to the mayor, although he is not as intimate with him as some secretaries have been with their mayors. Morgan and Lindsay, nevertheless, trust each other, and Morgan has served as an advisor to the mayor concerning city affairs. Unfortunately for Morgan, the deputy mayor has become much closer to the mayor than he has been able to and is much aware of the importance of the media to present the mayor and his policies successfully. Consequently, the deputy mayor often has interfered with and disrupted the functions of the press secretary.

The duties and responsibilities of the press secretary to the mayor of New York City have changed during the years that the office has been in existence. Originally, the press secretary was involved mostly with issuing press releases concerning events related to City Hall, to protect the mayor from the incessant probes of the working press, and to present a favorable image of the mayor and his programs to the press and ultimately the public. The success of the press secretary has always been based on his ability to deal skillfully with reporters and to gain their respect and trust. At present, the press secretary must be an able journalist, but he also must be a good politician and be sufficiently well informed to contribute extensively to determining the decisions the mayor will endorse. To do this successfully, he has to establish an intimate and personal relationship with the mayor and gain his trust and faith, for it has been demonstrated that the greater the degree of intimacy, the more effective he will be as press secretary. The position of press secretary now has a power base rooted solely in a personal trust between him and the mayor without any statutory legitimacy.

GLOSSARY

Attribution
: Press secretary or other spokesman can be quoted as having revealed information source.

Not for Attribution
: Permits government officials to talk freely to newsmen without being quoted. It is used to test public reaction to new schemes and projected appointments and to mobilize public opinion behind some government project. It permits greater flexibility in taking policy initiative without chancing the man's own reputation or that of his agency.

Background briefings
: Conferences with the working press and the press secretary to tell them what's behind a story; conferences with the chief executive, press secretary, commissioners and other departmental people involved to "warm up" the chief executive for the regular press conference.

Backgrounders	Newsmen can report what they are told but they cannot identify the source either by name or as a spokesman.
On deep deep background	You take the press into your confidence; you give them just enough to say without being quoted directly.
Communication drop-off	Misinformation or unwittingly received wrong information between two or more people.
Credibility gap	The bridge between fact and fiction in government release of news to the press.
Exclusive	Press secretary giving information or facts solely to one reporter and not another.
Feedback	Public response to news given in the media through tips, rumors, and trial balloon techniques.
Handouts	Press releases that are distributed gratuitously to the working press.
Leak	Press secretary or some other government official suggesting an idea or giving a tip to reporters on the side and not through a regular press release. This is usually done to test public reaction. (The public response is known as feedback.) The chief executive then decides to go ahead or not go ahead with his proposed policy or appointment.

Off-the-record   Press secretary or other government
                        official speaking to reporters with
                        the understanding that the information
                        being given is confidential and not to
                        be quoted.

Overnights   Press release distributed in the after-
                        noon for the next morning or after-
                        noon papers. It gives the media time
                        to plan out their assignments and
                        the press secretary to plan out some
                        of his work.

Press conference   Usually the question and answer
                        meeting with the chief executive, the
                        press, the press secretary and others
                        involved; the working press questions
                        the chief executive on matters of
                        current event especially as concerned
                        in government, the "give-and-take"
                        of the democratic process and the
                        "people's right to know."

Press release   Written news story that comes from
                        the press secretary's office and dis-
                        tributed to reporters, also known as
                        handout.

Put the lid on   This concludes a press briefing, and
                        the reporter is free to leave without
                        hesitation of missing a "hot" story.
                        This usually signifies the ending of a
                        press secretary briefing at the White
                        House until the hour for the next
                        one to begin.

Scoop yourself   Two or more stories in the same paper
                        or on television emanating from the
                        press secretary's office, both stories
                        "hot" and singularly important.

Spokesman	Usually the press secretary or other government official quoted in place of the chief executive. The chief executive may not be available or does not wish to be quoted directly but a particular person, usually the press secretary, may be authorized to make comment in his behalf.
Tips or rumors	Information that might be fact or fiction leading to a possible story or leak about a situation.
Trial balloon	Testing of a policy or idea or appointment through the media, possibly giving the story to a columnist other than a regular reporter.
Working press	Newsprint and broadcast journalists covering the daily news for the media. In this particular instance, those reporters assigned to City Hall by their papers and stations.
One upsmanship	Be "one ahead" of the reporter; have a good story ready to counteract a bad one.[2]

NOTES

CHAPTER ONE

1. Wallace S. Sayre and Herbert Kaufman, *Governing New York City* (New York: Russell Sage Foundation, 1960) pp. 668-669.

CHAPTER TWO

1. Harold C. Syrett, ed., *The Gentleman and the Tiger: The Autobiography of George B. McClellan, Jr.* (Philadelphia: Lippincott, 1956), p. 166.
2. Address, delivered in City Hall, Rochester, New York, and reported in the *Brooklyn Charter.*
3. Seth Low, "The Government of Cities in the United States," *The Century,* September 1891, p. 65.
4. Report of Special Committee No. 1505, *250th Anniversary of the Establishment of Municipal Government in the City of New Amsterdam* (1903).
5. Seth Low, *Scrapbooks* (New York: Municipal Archives).
6. Ibid.
7. Letter to the Society for the Prevention of Vice, United Charities Building, 105 East Twenty-second Street, New York City, January 23, 1902, responding to the Society's query concerning the enforcement of the Excise Law.

8. Low, op. cit.
9. Letter to Rev. Charles H. Parkhurst, President, Society for the Prevention of Vice, 133 East Thirty-fifth Street, New York City, dated January 23, 1902. Signed by the Secretary of the Mayor.
10. Elmer E. J. Cornwell, *Presidential Leadership of Public Opinion* (Bloomington: Indiana University Press, 1965), p. 15.
11. Syrett, op. cit., p. 184.
12. Ibid., p. 226.
13. Ibid., p. 192.
14. Ibid., p. 171.
15. Ibid., p. 176. (A recent example is the confrontation between President Richard Nixon and the national press. See *New York Times,* October 27, November 3, 1973.)
16. Ibid., pp. 280-281.
17. Ibid., p. 221.
18. Ibid., p. 224.
19. Ibid., pp. 250-251.
20. Ibid., pp. 250-251.
21. Ibid.
22. Ibid., p. 242.
23. Ibid., p. 187.
24. Ibid., pp. 188-189.
25. Ibid., p. 187.
26. Ibid., p. 186.
27. Ibid., p. 189.
28. Ibid.
29. Ibid., p. 200.
30. Ibid., p. 208.
31. Ibid.
32. Ibid., p. 189.
33. Ibid., p. 253.
34. Ibid., p. 267.
35. Ibid., pp. 271-272.
36. Ibid.
37. Ibid., pp. 317-318.
38. Ibid., pp. 272-273.
39. Ibid., p. 274.
40. Ibid., p. 301.
41. *The World,* January 16, 1910. "Aunt Kate Carow" (the statement was dictated at the end of the interview).
42. *Municipal Yearbook,* 1913, compiled and prepared by Robert Adamson, Secretary to the Mayor, the Mayor's Office, New York, July 19, 1913.

43. *New York Times,* August 20, 1913.
44. William Russell Hochman, *William J. Gaynor: The Years of Fruition* (unpublished doctoral dissertation, Columbia University, 1955), p. 216 (Doctoral Dissertation Series, Publication No. 12, 309).
45. Gaynor to the editor of the Annapolis *Capital,* June 18, 1910.
46. Gaynor to Paratt, April 18 and 21, 1910. Letters to Mr. Paratt, Secretary, New York Chamber of Commerce.
47. "Do Our Courts Stand in the Way of Social and Economic Justice, and if so, By What Authority" (address before the Yale Forum, Yale University, New Haven, Connecticut).
48. Hochman, op. cit., pp. 226-227; *American,* April 15, 1910.
49. *New York Times* (May 1, 1910).
50. *The World,* April 29, 1910. (Hearst had been a candidate for mayor in 1905, and for governor in 1906.)
51. *Evening Post,* April 29, 1910.
52. Gaynor, op. cit., pp. 30-31
53. Louis Heaton Pink, *Gaynor: The Tammany Mayor Who Swallowed The Tiger* (New York: International Press, 1933), p. 186.
54. Ibid., p. 186.
55. Ibid., p. 65.
56. Pink, op. cit., p. 66.
57. Pink, op. cit., pp. 66, 67.
58. Ibid., p. 243.
59. Ibid., p. 299.
60. Ibid.
61. Pink, op. cit., pp. 300-301.
62. Pink, op. cit., p. 190.
63. Mortimer Smith, *William J. Gaynor, Mayor of New York* (Chicago: Regency, 1951), pp. xix-xx.
64. William J. Gaynor, *Manuscripts and Mayoralty Papers* (New York City Municipal Archives).
65. Ibid.
66. Ibid.
67. Pink, op. cit., p. 71.
68. Pink, op. cit., p. 69.
69. William J. Gaynor, *Mayor Gaynor's Letters and Speeches* (New York: Greaves Publishing Co., 1913), p. 298.
70. Gaynor, *Manuscripts and Mayoralty Papers,* op. cit.
71. Hochman, op. cit., p. 504.
72. Gaynor, *Letters and Speeches,* op. cit., pp. 26-28.
73. Gaynor, *Letters and Speeches,* op. cit., p. 242.
74. Statement of Mayor Kline, dated October 3, 1913.

CHAPTER THREE

1. Speech at the Dinner of the Committee of 107 at the Hotel Astor, May 2, 1916.
2. Mayor John Purroy Mitchel, address delivered on May 2, 1916 to the Committee of 107.
3. Julian Street, "New York's Fighting Mayor," *Collier's,* August 24, 1917, p. 39.
4. Book 19, Mayor Mitchel's Letterpress Records.
5. Mayor John Purroy Mitchel, excerpts from address at the Lawyer's Club, March 17, 1917.
6. Letter dated June 3, 1915, written by the Acting Mayor George McAneny.
7. John Purroy Mitchel, "Why Our Tax Rate is High," Statement by the Honorable John Purroy Mitchel, Mayor of the City of New York, on the Tax Budget for 1916 and the Financial Policy of the City Administration, the *New York Herald,* October 3, 1915, pp. 4-5.
8. Mayor John P. Mitchel, statement to the press, August 13, 1914.
9. Ibid.
10. Mayor Mitchel, Scrapbook No. 7, item dated September 13, 1915.
11. Excerpts of remarks made at the luncheon of the Associated Press held at the Waldorf Asotria, April 21, 1914.
12. Address at the New York Press Club, April 17, 1914.
13. Address at the dinner of the Press Club at the Waldorf Astoria, June 30, 1916.
14. Remarks made at the dinner of the American Newspaper Publishers Association at the Waldorf Astoria on April 22, 1914.
15. Street, op. cit., p. 6.
16. Letterpress Book 19, op. cit., Press Interview, October 15, 1917 (Municipal Archives).
17. The speech mentioned was delivered before the Atlantic Deeper Waterways Association of New York. According to Mayor Mitchel, the papers had misquoted the speech and taken it out of context.
18. Excerpts of Remarks of Honorable John Purroy Mitchel at the City Hall. January 1, 1914, on assuming the office of Mayor of the City of New York.
19. Charles J. Rosebault, "Mitchel's Election a National Triumph." (New York: Public Welfare Committee, 50 East 42nd Street).
20. *In Memoriam* John Purroy Mitchel, 1879-1918, published by the Class of 1899, Columbia College, 1918. The quotations had been excerpted from New York City newspapers published during the week following Mayor Mitchel's death.

21. Ibid.
22. Ibid.
23. W. A. Swanberg, *Citizen Hearst* New York: Charles Scribner's Sons, 1961), pp. 332-333, 353.
24. Ibid., p. 338.
25. Epexegeticus, "John F. Hylan of New York", *Sketches of American Mayors,* pp. 161-162.
26. Ibid., p. 317.
27. New York *Journal,* September 15, 1922.
28. New York *Journal,* 1918.
29. Swanberg, op. cit., p. 315.
30. Ibid., pp. 162-163.
31. Ibid., p. 164.
32. Letter to Mayor Hylan, received from Thomas A. Farley, Democratic leader of the 14th Assembly District.
33. Mayor's Letter to Mr. Herbert C. Pell, Jr. Chairman, Democratic State Committee, 15 East 40th Street, New York, dated June 26, 1925.
34. Address at a meeting of Departments, City Hall, June 22, 1925.
35. John Hylan, statement by the Mayor, City of New York, dated July 2, 1925.
36. John Francis Hylan, *Autobiography of John Francis Hylan, Mayor of New York* (New York: The Rotary Press, 1922), authorized edition.
37. Address at dinner of American Institute of Homeopathy at Roosevelt Hotel, June 25, 1925.
38. Address at the Municipal Building, New York, July 8, 1925.
39. Remarks by Mayor John F. Hylan, at the Dinner Conference of Law Enforcing Departments of the City of New York, held at the Waldorf-Astoria, October 6, 1920.
40. Swanberg, op. cit., p. 379.
41. Ibid.
42. Mayor John F. Hylan's Letter to Hon. Royal S. Copeland, 250 West 57th Street, New York City, dated August 25, 1925.
43. The *Subway Sun* consisted of subway advertisement posters and placards.
44. *The ABC of Hylanism,* Pamphlet published for mayoral campaign of 1925.
45. *New York American,* September 17, 1925.
46. Author's interpretation.

CHAPTER FOUR

1. Louis J. Gribetz and Joseph Kaye, *Jimmy Walker: The Story of a Personality* (New York: Dial Press, 1932), p. 224.
2. Ibid.
3. The *New York Times,* January 23, 1926.
4. Gene Fowler, *Beau James* (New York: Viking Press, 1949), p. 167.
5. Meyer Berger, *The Story of The New York Times 1851-1951* (New York: Simon and Schuster, 1951), p. 350.
6. Fowler, op. cit., p. 212.
7. Henry F. Pringle, "Jimmy Walker," The *American Mercury,* Vol. IX, No. 35, November 1926, p. 279.
8. *New York Times,* May 14, 1928.
9. Fowler, op. cit., p. 244.
10. Gribetz and Kaye, op. cit., p. 143.
11. Pringle, op. cit., p. 275.
12. Joseph D. McGoldrick, "Our American Mayors—Jimmy Walker," *National Municipal Review,* Vol. XVII, No. 10, October 1928, p. 574.
13. Gribetz and Kaye, op. cit., p. 277.
14. Ibid., p. 48.
15. New York City Municipal Archives, Scrapbooks of Mayor James J. Walker.
16. New York City Municipal Archives, Mayor's Scrapbooks; also Gribetz and Kaye, op. cit. p. 202.
17. Gribetz and Kaye, op. cit., p. 216.
18. Ibid., p. 240.
19. Hector Fuller, *Abroad with Mayor Walker* (New York: Shields Publishing Company, , 928), p. 61.
20. Ibid., p. 234.
21. Ibid., p. 23.
22. Fuller, op. cit., p. 101
23. New York City Municipal Archives, Scrapbooks of Mayor James J. Walker.
24. Herbert Mitgang, *The Man Who Rode the Tiger* (Philadelphia: Lippincott, 1962), pp. 246-247.
25. Ibid., p. 176.
26. Ibid., p. 168.
27. Ibid., p. 171.
28. *New York Times,* May 26, 1932.
29. *New York Daily News,* May 26, 1932.
30. *New York Times,* May 27, 1932.

31. *New York Times,* June 3, 1932.
32. Fowler, op. cit., p. 327.
33. Ibid., p. 328.
34. Mitgang, op. cit., p. 345.
35. Ibid.
36. *New York Times,* September 3, 1932.
37. This information was obtained in an interview with Frank Doyle, press secretary to Mayor Wagner, March 1, 1971.
38. Telephone interviews with Emanuel Perlmutter, *New York Times* reporter, March 1971; May 1972.
39. Ibid.
40. Arthur Mann, *LaGuardia Comes to Power* (Philadelphia: J. B. Lippincott Company, 1965), p. 90.
41. Ibid., p. 121.

CHAPTER FIVE

1. The F. H. LaGuardia Papers, stored in the Municipal Archives and Records, contain correspondence, memoranda, newspaper clippings, congressional bills, campaign posters and leaflets, photographs, manuscripts and reprints of speeches, articles, and press releases.
2. Fiorello H. LaGuardia, *The Making of an Insurgent* (Philadelphia: J. B. Lippincott. 1948), pp. 29-30.
3. Jay Franklin, *LaGuardia: A Biography* (New York: The Macmillan Company, 1945), p. 48.
4. *New York Times,* October 24, 1933.
5. Joseph McKee, "A Serious Problem . . . On The Importance of Catholic Education," reprinted in *The Paulist Press,* New York, p. 4, 1915.
6. *New York Evening World,* November 8, 1933.
7. *New York Evening Post,* November 8, 1933.
8. Municipal Archives, LaGuardia Scrapbooks.
9. Paul J. Kern, "Fiorello H. LaGuardia," in J. T. Slater, Editor, *The American Soldier* (Chapel Hill: The University of North Carolina Press, 1938), pp. 152-153.
10. Paul B. Weston, *A Hammer in the City* (Evanston: Regency Books, 1962), p. 58.
11. Kern, op. cit., p. 185.
12. Ibid.
13. Interview with Mrs. Ruth Stone, widow of Lester Stone, November 1970.

14. Ernest Cuneo, *Life with Fiorello* (New York: The Macmillan Company, 1955), pp. 73-74.
15. Kern, op. cit., p. 28.
16. Municipal Archives, LaGuardia Scrapbook.
17. Interview with Irving Spiegel, April 1971.
18. Weston, op. cit., p. 70.
19. Municipal Archives, LaGuardia Scrapbooks.
20. Weston, op. cit., p. 133.
21. LaGuardia Radio Broadcasts, May 7, 1944, pp. 8-9.
22. LaGuardia Radio Broadcasts, October 28, 1945, p. 12.
23. LaGuardia Radio Broadcasts, February 18, 1945, pp. 5-6.
24. LaGuardia Radio Broadcasts, April 18, 1943.
25. Ibid., pp. 150-151.
26. LaGuardia Radio Broadcasts, December 2, 1945, p. 4.
27. LaGuardia Radio Broadcasts, November 18, 1945, p. 11.
28. LaGuardia Radio Broadcasts, November 11, 1945.
29. LaGuardia Radio Broadcasts, November 12, 1944.
30. LaGuardia Radio Broadcasts, November 5, 1944.
31. LaGuardia Radio Broadcasts, June 10, 1945.
32. LaGuardia Radio Broadcasts, November 11, 1945.
33. Municipal Archives, LaGuardia Scrapbooks.
34. LaGuardia Radio Broadcasts.
35. *New York World Telegram,* October 12, 1933.
36. LaGuardia Radio Braodcasts, December 30, 1945, p. 3.
37. Municipal Archives, LaGuardia Scrapbooks.
38. *New York Times.* January 2, 1938.
39. Franklin, op. cit., p. 163.

CHAPTER SIX

1. Statement by former Vincent Impellitteri, Interview, June 22, 1972, New York City.
2. Interview with Gabe Pressman, March 1971.
3. Room at New York City Hall assigned to newspapermen.
4. *New York Times,* May 5, 1948.
5. Mayor's Committee for the Commemoration of the Golden Anniversary of the City of New York, Press Release, May 12, 1948.
6. Ibid.
7. *New York Times,* August 17, 1948.
8. *New York Times,* September 15, 1948.

9. *The New York Sun,* November 1, 1948.
10. *New York Times,* November 3, 1948.
11. *New York Times,* June 21, 1972, p. 46 (obituary of Frank MacMaster.
12. New York City Municipal Archives. Wire Service Press Clips, Mayor William O'Dwyer.
13. Interview with former Mayor Vincent Impellitteri, June 22, 1972.

CHAPTER SEVEN

1. *New York World Telegram,* September 1950.
2. Interview with former Mayor Vincent Impellitteri, June 22, 1972.
3. Ibid. (Mayor Impellitteri emphasized this point.)
4. New York City Municipal Archives, Wire Service Press Clips.
5. Ibid.

CHAPTER EIGHT

1. Interview with William Peer, January 1971.
2. Interview with Frank Doyle, March 1971.
3. Emphasis is added to point up the commanding aspects of the position as demonstrated by the mayor in his order to his executive secretary.
4. *New York Times,* February 1, 1971.
5. *New York Times,* February 3, 1971.
6. Interview with Timothy J. Cooney, March 1971, New York City. Sadly, I had waited for Debs Myers to recuperate from his illness to interview him, but Myers died while I was interviewing in Europe in February 1971. I was privileged, however, to interview Tim Cooney, one of his assistants, in New York, who had heard of my study on press secretaries.
7. Interview with Emanuel Perlmutter, March 1971, May 1972. This was the first time the title press secretary was officially used.
8. Interview with Leslie Slote, January 1971.
9. Interview with Paul Bragdon, New York, November 1971.
10. Interview with Jeffrey Roche, December 1970.
11. Interview with Warren Moscow, December 1970.
12. Telephone interviews with Emmanuel Perlmutter, *New York Times* reporter, March 1971; May 1972.

CHAPTER NINE

1. Woody Klein, *Lindsay's Promise: The Dream that Failed* (New York: The Macmillan Company, 1970), pp. 18-19.
2. Ibid.
3. Ibid., pp. 24, 69.
4. Interview with Harry O'Donnell, November, December, 1970.
5. *New York Times Magazine,* "The Lindsay Inner Circle," October 15, 1967, p. 108.
6. Interview with Thomas Morgan, March 1971.
7. Interview with Robert Laird, November 1970.
8. Allard Lowenstein is a reform democrat and was an old 19th district New York Congressman who had lost his bid for reelection.

CHAPTER TEN

1. Interview with Joe Breu, March 1971.
2. Interview with Richard Reeves, March 1971.
3. Interview with Gabe Pressman, March 1971.
4. Interview with Harry O'Donnell, November-December 1970.

INDEX